Sh

Four Simple Questions to Help You Resolve Shame and Feel Understood

Dolan Mayeda

www.shamehack.com

For information, contact www.shamehack.com.
Shame Hack™, Four Simple Questions™, and Healing Dialogue™ are trademarks of Dolan Mayeda.

All names in case studies have been changed to protect the privacy of the individuals involved.

The information and resources contained in this book are for informational purposes only and are not intended to assess, diagnose, or treat any medical and/or mental health disease or condition. The author does not imply nor establish any type of therapist-client relationship with readers. Furthermore, the information obtained from this book should not be considered a substitute for a thorough medical and/or mental health evaluation by an appropriately credentialed and licensed professional.

The testimonials included in this book are not necessarily representative of everyone who uses Shame Hack; individual results may vary. The author does not warrant or guarantee a particular outcome.

ISBN: 0-9960724-0-3
Cover Art and Graphic Design by Teresa Espaniola
Photography by Monica Royal
Edited by Lerissa Patrick

To my Dad

Because everyone deserves to feel understood

&

Tempe

Forever in our hearts

Acknowledgements

To my parents, Dennis and Beatrice, the safety net that allowed me to try, fail, and succeed, whose love and support mean so much. To Dr. Timothy Francis, who taught me so much about the body and healing. When we first met he told me "letters don't make the doctor." I haven't forgotten. My mentor Kathleen, who taught me about feelings and love. Dr. Bertrand Faucret for his sustained enthusiasm.

Deep gratitude to the wonderful people who allowed me to share their stories.

Thank you to my editors: Leslie Rankin, who got a book out of me and was patient and kind when I was clueless; Tracy Jones, who helped me find my voice; Lerissa Patrick, for helping me get to the finish line. Melissa Morgan your eye for detail especially with ellipsis and your quick turnaround times.

A special thank you to Anne Clarkin, who was my ballast when I felt like I was sinking. I appreciate all your contributions, and especially your willingness to be my sounding board. Leah Gregory for all the time she spent hashing out concepts for this book. Tamara Merrill for her suggestions and many beta reads.

Dr. Darrick Sahara for fixing me up when my health went goofy. Tim Erickson, who saved me when my computer showed me the blue screen of death.

A sincere thank you to all the people who participated in the beta read. I appreciate your honest feedback.

My family for your love and support.

Renee, Bailey, Emily, Terry, Jerelyn and Marky for all your support and cooking when my dad got sick. Thank you so much for being there.

A.G.: Thank you for all of your encouragement.

Mike Kim and Charlie Middleton, both of whom I've known since kindergarten: Thank you for your friendship over all these years. That goes for Brit and Mike D as well.

Gall, Sattler, Rach, Bird, and Marceau for having my back.

Jamie, Vince, Chris, Javier, Greg, Sean, Drew, and Marla for your generosity.

Michelle, Rich, Juli, Mike, Donn, Bill, Patty, Moze, and Miles for your love and support.

Lastly, thank you to my patients. I am honored and grateful that you allowed me to practice the healing arts.

Oh and Karma, I hope this makes us even.

TABLE OF CONTENTS

Shame Hack *noun* **1** An unusually clever resolution to the painful feeling of not being enough **2** A short cut to overturning what makes you feel like you're not enough **3** A method of discovering what lies deep in your heart **4** A way to work on yourself without involving your story **5** A quick shift from feeling sad, hurt, angry, fear, or shame **6** A resolution to a feeling that's been bothering you **7** A way to help you feel understood

verb **1** To change the way you experience yourself **2** To discover your truth **3** To discover meaning, direction, and purpose by resolving shame **4** To demonstrate to your heart that you understand how it feels

Introduction

In order to understand shame one must have experienced deep shame and confronted it sufficiently to have assimilated it personally, and pursued it cognitively wherever it led, and finally, to have the courage to risk further shame by exposing oneself in writing.

-Silvan S. Tomkins – Developer of Affect Theory

I am probably the last person you'd expect to write a self-help book. In fact, I never set out to write a self-help book. I'm not an academic with 32 gigs of data and research to support my position. I'm not a therapist with hundreds of case studies. I'm not even a writer; writing has always been a challenge. So who am I? I am a chiropractic kinesiologist, of 14 years, living and helping clients in San Diego. I'm also a seasoned participant of multiple years in therapy, both group and individual. And that's where my voyage to Shame Hack™ began.

In 2004 I was living with my girlfriend. We fought constantly; I'd never been in a relationship so toxic before. I was unhappy and dissatisfied. My life just wasn't working very well, and I wanted it to change. So when a client suggested I attend a three-day intensive workshop she was facilitating, I decided to go. I was intrigued by this client; she was matter-of-fact about her childhood molestation, and she always seemed to find me when I retreated to my usual conversational hiding spaces.

The workshop was an intense emotional experience. I learned all about childhood wounds and inner child therapy – information I didn't have before. I was flying high for a good two weeks after the workshop, and impressed with my genuine sense of happiness. But my relationship still wasn't working. We broke up, and I decided I needed more help. I entered group therapy.

It was there that I gradually broke my habit of suppressing my feelings and learned to feel them instead. It was there that I talked with a doll to find my "inner child." And it was in talking to my doll that I discovered shame. My first time talking with the doll, my tone shocked me: I sounded impatient and irritated and my voice dripped contempt. This, I learned, was the voice of shame.

What is the Meaning?

Having met shame, I was eager to get to the bottom of it. But the weeks in therapy turned into months, and the months into years, and still I felt unworthy. *Where does shame end?* I asked myself. It seemed as if I was suffering for suffering's sake. *I'm feeling shame for no reason with no end in sight. There's no meaning. There's no light at the end of this tunnel,* I thought. *It's not a tunnel. It's a cave.* The benefits of feeling my feelings had reached a plateau.

In frustration, I began to play around with ways of getting at the meaning in my feelings. I started with this statement: **The fact that I feel shame means ______**. So when I failed at something and I felt shame, I would think, *the fact I feel shame means success is important to me. All I am doing is trying my best, despite coming up short. I keep trying ... wait ... I'm not a failure! I'm thinking about this wrong. What I really am is* ***determined****. That's the truth. I am determined.*

As I worked with that statement, my shame stopped! I was ecstatic! It was like rays of sunshine beaming through thick clouds and angelic choirs singing. And to my surprise, I felt understood.

But I can be a bit skeptical. My joy seemed too good to be true. *Am I being pranked? Can this be happening?* I thought. Checking inside, I knew it was real. *I can feel it. I can feel the difference. I don't feel shame anymore.*

I decided to try again to make sure this wasn't a fluke. The next time I felt shame, I ran through the "meaning statement," and sure enough, the shame disappeared.

It may be hard to believe that a simple statement can be so powerful. But I'm living proof that it is.

The Four Simple Questions™

I did this over and over, working, tinkering, and improving the "meaning statement." Eventually, it evolved into its final form: The Four Simple Questions. They are:

What Am I Feeling?

What Did I Make That Mean?

What Does That Say About Me?

What's the Truth?

Now, every time I feel shame, I answer the Four Simple Questions and *click!* More peace and understanding. *Click! Click! Click!* Peace and understanding spreads across my inner landscape. My critical twin is cleaving off.

What has this meant for my life?

It has changed how I experience myself. I believed I was unlovable, for one thing. Shame Hack helped me know that *I am lovable,* and this has colored my entire experience. I act differently. I no longer live in fear of someone hurting me, scared someone will provoke my feelings of unworthiness. I've grown calmer and more settled. My confidence has grown, and my anxiety has faded. I enjoy myself more!

While I consider myself liberated from shame, I'm not immune to it. Shame still bites me every now and again. But now, I deal with it completely differently than I did in the past. Now I use it to further my insight and intuition. Shame is not my boss; it is my servant. *It* works for *me* now.

Now I can feel understood. Feeling understood is a basic need. But for me and (perhaps you) this basic need has largely and painfully gone unmet.

Not anymore. To my surprise, I discovered that feeling understood is something I can create within myself. Feeling understood isn't completely dependent on another person when you can demonstrate to your heart that *you* understand how it feels. You feel understood.

Teaching Shame Hack

Early in my career, I was shocked and heartbroken to hear how much abuse and emotional trauma my patients had experienced. I had heard about childhood abuse and sexual assaults and read the statistics, but when I came face to face with it in real life, it became personal.

My clients were good people whom I came to care about. They were loving, beautiful, generous, caring, good-hearted people selling themselves short at every turn. I knew there was so much more to them, but their shame ran deep. They were filled with disheartening feelings; they were convinced they were unworthy, unlovable, and unacceptable, and that they didn't belong. These feelings were driving them. They affected every part of life, from relationships and parenting to their self-esteem and enjoyment of their accomplishments.

I helped them as best I could, but I wanted to do more. They were being robbed of hope and love, and there was only one reason: They didn't know how to deal with their deep shame. They needed a tool to help them cope with their feelings instead of shutting them down or stuffing them away, because these unresolved feelings just ended up adversely affecting their health in some other way.

When I developed Shame Hack, I decided to see if it would work for my clients - and it did.

Then it occurred to me that I could reach more people if I held Shame Hack classes rather than just one-to-one teaching. That worked, too - people learned it in class.

Finally, I wondered if people could learn Shame Hack from a book. So I wrote this book.

This Book is For You

I wrote this book with you in mind, dear reader. You don't know it yet but I'm your biggest cheerleader. I'm here to help and hopefully, liberate you from shame so that you can live your fullest, most content and authentic life.

This book is for you. The unease you feel in your heart, the discomfort, the tension, is like an arrow in a drawn bow waiting to be released. The arrow already knows its target and path before you ever release it. So does your heart.

Let fly the arrow! Liberate your heart - it already knows where it's headed.

There's nothing to wait for! Let's go.

Part 1: Getting Ready

Part 1 contains the "prep work" you need to do before you try the Shame Hack. You'll need to learn (if you don't already know) how to feel your feelings, how to identify shame, and some of the principles behind The Four Simple Questions.

Flowcharts and worksheet available at:
www.shamehack.com/flowcharts

Chapter 1: One Mind

There are so many ideas and experiences of shame. Everybody is coming from their own place. It's important to clear up any confusion and make sure we're talking about the same thing. For a productive discussion, we need to become of one mind about the subject. This way we'll be thinking about it in the same way.

Shame Hack approaches shame as purely an emotion. Shame is something you feel. There are other ways to think about it, such as psychological, social, cultural, and biological phenomena. But our approach is to treat shame simply as a feeling.

With this one mind, let's talk about what shame feels like. First of all, it's painful. The pain can be excruciating, like a rhinoceros stepping on your chest. And it feels like you are not enough. You're less-than. You're the only one.

This space of not measuring up, isolation, and being inherently flawed is the place we'll be coming from.

When shame runs deep to your core, it can get ugly. It casts a hue of self-loathing. You feel you are bad. Not bad like Michael Jackson bad. But bad as in worthless, pathetic. You don't deserve to breathe. You're just taking up space and using up resources. No one loves you. No one cares, and why should they? You're not worthy. You're not wanted. You're not precious. There's something wrong with you. It's a hurtful existence.

Then as you live, your life experiences reinforce this distorted belief, creating a downward spiral. You feel unworthy. It must be true. How do you know it's true? Because you feel this way. Away you go.

Doing your best to combat these corrosive feelings, you look for relief. The feelings can be overwhelming and unbearable. You please people. You retreat to your inner world. You lose yourself in relationships. You become controlling. You freeze. Perhaps you take more extreme measures you: drink, eat, cut, starve, have sex, gamble, self-medicate, or shop the feelings away. But these behaviors don't make the shame go away. Instead, you are taken hostage by the inner emotional terrorist.

The Price of Shame

Why did I write this book? This book is here because the cost you pay for shame is too high.

I believe in challenging shame. Shame has robbed you of feeling worthy. Shame has robbed you of feeling loved, feeling comfortable in your own skin. Shame has taken so much from you. It's time to take back what's yours and heal the shame you feel inside.

Sometimes, when shame runs deep, it's hard to feel loved, to let people love and accept the real you, warts and all. Making intimate connections can be especially difficult. Exposure! Ahhh! Letting love in can be scary. Love can be hard to trust. Perhaps love is even painful, especially if you've been wronged, hurt or scarred by someone in your past.

You need to feel safe in order to let love in. Feeling loved begins with you. This is why self-love is such a big part of Shame Hack. I'm not talking the pampering kind of love, such as a Gucci bag, manicures and pedicures, massages, or wine. Those are all well and good but those fleeting pleasures do not get through to your heart.

I'm talking about the kindness and love that would touch the heart of a hurting two-year old. You fill a toddler's heart with caring attention. A two-year old is not impressed with a Gucci bag. A two-year old wants to feel understood and so do you. Kindness, love, and attention are what soothe a hurting heart.

Healing your heart and resolving shame occur when two conditions are met:

You show your heart you know how it feels.

You find meaning in your suffering.

Showing your heart you know how it feels helps you feel understood.

Finding the meaning in your suffering changes its very nature, bringing it to resolution. Achieving both of these two conditions is what Shame Hack is founded on.

Your Truth

Shame Hack in its entirety is the Four Simple Questions plus the Healing Dialogue. We go into detail about these two parts later in the book. Here are the Four Simple Questions:

1. What am I feeling?
2. What did I make that mean?
3. What does that say about me?
4. What's the truth?

The Four Simple Questions lead you step by step from feeling shame to finding your truth. Your truth is the answer to Question 4. Your truth is usually an *I am* statement, such as *I am lovable* or *I am worthy*. Your truth is what overturns a shameful, distorted belief and fills a hole in your heart.

Let's say you work through the Four Simple Questions and discover your truth is: *I am generous.* Before your discovery, your shame drove you. You believed yourself cheap, selfish or unsuccessful. You engaged in compulsive giving. You overextended and overcommitted yourself. You tried to prove to yourself and other people that you were selfless and generous. Your attempts to prove yourself helped you avoid shame. You gave and gave.

When you realize your truth - I *am generous* - you know in your heart that you *are* generous. You no longer have to overextend or overcommit and bankrupt yourself financially or emotionally. You can save something for yourself and your loved ones. You have nothing to prove. You *know* you are generous and that's enough. You are enough. You can establish and maintain a boundary more easily this way.

Shame Hack vs. Shame Cure

Shame Hack is not a cure. It's not the end-all/be-all. You will not go through Shame Hack once, answer the Four Simple Questions and never feel shame again. That's not going to happen.

Here's what's more likely to happen. You go through Shame Hack and reclaim a piece of yourself. You grow stronger and more confident and feel understood in the process. You familiarize yourself with shame and recognize it sooner. Your self-compassion and authenticity blossom. With each reclaimed piece of yourself you grow a little more whole. Piece by piece, the mosaic of who you are falls into place. A new you starts taking shape. Your feelings become a little less overwhelming. Meaningful connection becomes a little easier to establish.

Shame Hack is not a cure. It's a tool. It's a life skill.

What is Shame Hack?

Shame Hack is "feel your feelings" with a twist. If you're unfamiliar with the term "feel your feelings," not to worry. There's a chapter dedicated to it. For now, just understand that feeling your feelings is allowing yourself to experience your emotions unencumbered. As you feel your emotions unencumbered, you answer the Four Simple Questions. That's the twist.

Shame Hack deals with how you feel with regard to a recent, specific situation. It focuses on how you feel now. For example: Imagine you got talked over in a work meeting. It's bothering you. You have feelings about it. You'll take a closer look at what you're feeling with regard to getting talked over. Your feelings about getting talked over are the material you use when answering the Four Simple Questions. Since Shame Hack deals with what you feel now, when you resolve the feelings, you feel relief *now*.

You won't be looking at your childhood unless it comes up. Your childhood is not a focal point. What you may find is some feelings that come up are reminiscent of your childhood. You've felt the same way when you were a child.

Shame Hack is a feelings-driven process. You'll be using the wisdom of your body to guide you. When you react with your truth, it resonates. You feel it. There's no denying that the wisdom of your body is speaking to you. Feeling the truth in your body helps with visceral certainty, taking your head out of the equation.

The focus of Shame Hack is between you and your feelings. It's between you and your heart. Shame Hack is all about you - what you feel and what your feelings mean to you.

Shame Hack is an introspective process. But that doesn't mean you have to do it alone. You can if you wish. But sometimes it's helpful to go through it with someone else. This is especially true if you have deep shame or a history of trauma. If you're disconnected with your feelings, another person can help you sort through that. A mental health professional can help guide and support you through Shame Hack, too. From a human perspective, it's nice to be seen when you're up to your nostrils in shame. Having someone there to acknowledge and validate you can in itself be healing.

What Shame Hack is Not

Shame Hack is not a process for rationalizing your feelings away. It's more of a process for recognizing shame and stepping into it. Shame Hack is not here to address a complex, interwoven, multi-connected, multi-sourced entanglement phenomenon that happens to you. We're going to keep it simple and treat shame as a feeling only.

Shame Hack's approach is not about seeking empathy from other people. Receiving empathy from another person is a wonderful thing, and by all means continue with those validating conversations. It's just not the approach we are taking here.

For Shame Hack, you'll be giving yourself empathy and compassion. The only person that knows exactly how you feel – the depth, impact, pain, nuance and significance – is you. You are the only one who has been there every second of your life. People can relate and empathize, both of which feel fantastic and affirming. However, when someone fails to understand how you feel, it's okay, because you understand yourself. You can make yourself feel understood.

Shame Hack is not about "your story." Your story is the personal narrative about why you feel the way you do. It's courageous to share your story. Your story is important. And you will not share your story over and over, desensitizing yourself while you tell it. Your story is not the focus here. What you feel and its meaning is the focus. Focusing on what you feel and what it means to you oftentimes bypasses your story.

The Power of the Hack

What makes Shame Hack so powerful?

Shame Hack helps you uncover your values

Shame Hack gives you freedom

Shame Hack is a tool for life

Shame Hack shifts you at a core level

Shame Hack is fast

Shame Hack helps you feel understood

Shame Hack is simple

Shame Hack is powered by self-love

Gaining some control over your emotions is satisfying. Having a reliable tool to deal with and recover from unpleasant or painful feelings is a necessity. Instead of just suffering from unpleasant feelings, you resolve them.

Your feelings help uncover your values. You learn what makes your heart quiver, soar, or sing. When you connect with your heart, it becomes your compass. Your heart can help guide you when you feel lost.

Shame Hack gives you freedom. You don't have to live in fear of your feelings. Practicing the Four Simple Questions results in a natural increased tolerance of unpleasant feelings. In other words, when you use Shame Hack with any regularity, you can handle unpleasant feelings better. Just as you get stronger from regular physical exercise, you become more adept at dealing with unpleasant feelings with routine Shame Hack use.

Shame Hack is portable. It's available for you on demand. Maybe you need it when you visit your in-laws. No problem. Maybe you need it before a social situation. It's there for you. Maybe you go through a breakup. No worries.

Shame Hack is a tool for life. As your feelings change and evolve, Shame Hack goes right along with you. You will have feelings for the rest of your life. Shame Hack will be by your side.

Shame Hack changes you at a core level. Your truth shifts how you feel about yourself. You only need to take your truth to heart, making change come from the inside out.

Shame Hack is fast. When you discover your truth, the shift is immediate. You experience relief from feeling sad, hurt, anger, fear or shame. Going through Shame Hack doesn't take long. With practice, it's not unusual to complete the Four Simple Questions in less than an hour.

Shame Hack helps you feel understood. You can finally get this basic need met regularly. You understand what's been driving your patterns in a way that makes sense. You accept how you feel, and by doing this you accept yourself. Acceptance can often times feel like love.

Shame Hack develops your authenticity. You become more comfortable with yourself and your feelings. Your confidence grows because you have a better sense of who you are. You relate to people with authentic compassion because you've been there too.

Shame Hack is simple. It's not complicated. You just need to be honest with yourself. Feel your feelings, and your truth will resonate. That's it. When your heart is hurting, give it Healing Dialogue. Tell your heart the words it needs to hear.

The most powerful element of Shame Hack is that it's driven by self-love. You want your shame to end. You want to change how you feel. You want deeper connection. You want more for yourself. And you don't want just these things. You're willing to feel how your heart feels—even if it feels terrible, painful, or lonely—to get them. You're willing to be emotionally honest and accept how you feel. You're willing to plant a stake in the ground and say, "I am worth suffering for." You're willing to take action. You're taking responsibility for your heart and, as a result, it strengthens.

Making a stand for yourself communicates value, and love. This message of worth resonates with your heart. Your willingness resonates in a way your heart feels. Validating your worth shifts your heart from shame to something whole.

These heart-driven wants are what make Shame Hack powerful. You are putting your heart into it. Your heart brings the power. You are more powerful than shame will ever be.

A Little Getting Used To

Shame Hack is like getting a new pair of shoes. First you have to try them on to see if they fit. Sometimes with new shoes there's a breaking-in period. Shame Hack is the same: you need to see if Shame Hack is a good fit, and there might be a breaking-in period before you are comfortable.

The way the Four Simple Questions asks you to think may be foreign to you. It may take a couple of times before you get the gist of what the questions are asking for. Different ideas sometimes take a little getting used to.

Hopefully, Shame Hack will be a good fit for you. If not, that's okay! You can find another approach that helps you address shame. **What's most important is that you find a way to address shame that works for you**. Shame Hack is one tool, not the only tool. Shame is such an individual thing; it's hard to predict exactly what will work for you. This is why I encourage you to give Shame Hack a shot. Try it on and see if it works for you.

Where should we begin? With the Basics, of course. The Basics are the foundational concepts that Shame Hack is built upon.

My clients have generously offered to share some of their stories and experiences using Shame Hack. This is Rebecca's story.

Rebecca: A Priceless Tool

I am deeply grateful for the emotional healing process Dolan guided me through. It was incredibly transformative in a short amount of time. When I came in to see Dolan, I was desperate for help. I was experiencing an emotional crisis and was suffering paralyzing anxiety and fear, deep emotional sadness. I had been diagnosed with severe depression and anxiety and prescribed strong psychiatric medications that gave me a host of uncomfortable side effects and didn't relieve my emotional pain. I wasn't surprised the medication didn't really work. I knew the healing I was in search of would come from a holistic approach and involve releasing emotions that were held in my body.

When I came to his office, Dolan provided a very safe space for me to feel some intense emotions and assisted me through his process to get to the gift on the other side. By the end of our session, I felt calmer, more centered, and more grounded. The extreme fear I was feeling had subsided considerably. Just two days later I am feeling much calmer and more like myself again. Dolan is very compassionate, caring, and generous, and he is passionate about helping people heal on all levels and truly come to know themselves better. His process is helping me to integrate what I've learned about myself and it's a priceless tool that I can use on my own to grow. I felt heard, acknowledged, honored, and respected for who I am as a person and I've learned to be more compassionate with myself. I appreciate that Dolan has also practiced his tools in his own life, so he can relate to his patients and his understanding comes through in his work. That makes a huge difference.

With gratitude,
Rebecca

Chapter 2 – The Basics

In my final year of chiropractic school, I had a mentor. I met him for coffee as often as possible. He was (and is!) a brilliant guy, a walking, talking encyclopedia. His heart is pure gold. I respect him and admire his professional accomplishments.

Whenever we got together, I liked to pick his brain. I was getting ready to graduate and I wanted to learn all about the fancy, shiny healing stuff, the stuff that got the ooh's and aah's. But my mentor was big into the Basics. He liked to tell me, "Dolan, do the Basics. Do the Basics. Dolan, do the Basics. And did I tell you already, do the Basics."

One day, I started asking him about the latest miracle patients in the office – the difficult or interesting cases, the ones no one else seemed able to fix. "How did you fix them?" I asked. That day, he didn't want to give it up. Instead of a clinical pearl, he gave me a pearl of wisdom I'm happy to share with you:

As legend had it, in the ancient martial arts schools there were only two belt colors: white and black. You wore a white belt when you began your training. As you continued training, your white belt got dirtier and dirtier, eventually turning black. A black belt meant that you had the Basics down. You had put in the time and effort to master the foundational concepts. And only then, when you had a solid foundation to build upon, did you start learning what the art is all about.

# # #

A fundamental premise of Shame Hack is: Your feeling = Your responsibility. For example, perhaps your partner continues to do something that pisses you off even though you've asked him or her thirty-seven times to stop. You think: *Why can't he just change? I'm not asking for the world on a silver platter here.*

Your partner may not have the will, want, or capacity to change. People only change when *they* are ready and willing (no matter how hard you try). What's the only change *you* control? Changing how you feel about the behavior, situation or person. Sorry to have be the messenger here: Your feelings = Your responsibility. But here is the upside: That also means that Your responsibility = Your solution. Change is within your power. And the three Basics depend on your acceptance of this premise.

The following three foundational concepts are the Basics, plain and simple. They're what you need to know. These foundational concepts may seem obvious, so obvious that you overlook them. But don't. Get the Basics down first. They help you bypass your emotional defenses. Mastering the Basics is the first step in lifting the shame that weighs you down.

The three Basics are:

1. There's No Shame in Your Feelings
2. There's Meaning in Your Suffering
3. Only You Can Heal Yourself

There's No Shame in Your Feelings

This concept is as simple and straightforward as it seems (but often easier said than done). This basic means: Accept how you feel.

Let that sit for a minute. There's no shame in how you feel, none. Discovering there was no shame in my feelings came as a complete surprise to me. What an epiphany!

On my path to the Four Simple Questions, I kept trying to feel shame at deeper and deeper levels. I was trying to get to the root of my problems with connection, feeling my feelings, being understood, intimacy and, well, the list went on and on with shame behind them all. One inspired day, I tried to feel shame as deeply as I could. I wanted to see if I could feel shame all the way down to the nucleus of my cells. And there it was. Shame was in my DNA. (I go into more detail of this story in a later chapter.)

This discovery led me to conclude that if shame, like other feelings, is in my DNA, then I can't help that I feel it. I don't control my genetics. It's not my fault I feel shame. It's part of my wiring. I can't help it. There's nothing wrong with me! I'm normal. This is where the concept, "there's no shame in your feelings" comes from. You're normal if you feel shame. Nature intended you to have feelings.

But having feelings *about* your feelings is unnecessary. You might not like how you feel. But there is no need to get mad that you're mad. Or sad that you're mad. Or mad that you're sad. You get the idea. Having feelings about your feelings can cloud what you truly feel deep down. End the confusion and accept how you feel.

Keep it simple: If you feel mad, then own it. If you feel sad, then own it. If you feel shame, then own that, too.

You may have multiple feelings about a situation. Let's say you just got a new job offer. You might feel both happy and sad about it. Happy to advance your career, sad to leave behind your coworkers. Just avoid the "sad that you're sad" or "mad that you're sad" part. Accept how you feel at face value. Accepting how you feel is an important part of accepting yourself.

There's Meaning in Your Suffering

The path to the Four Simple Questions led me down the conventional routes. Individual therapy. Group therapy. A variety of workshops, seminars, and retreats on personal development. My self-help book shelf was small but classic. I incorporated meditation. I journaled. I even wrote with my non-dominant hand to express my inner child. Fading Post-it notes with mantras and positive thoughts cluttered my home and bathroom mirror.

Guess what? I still felt shame.

Feeling shame was getting old. I was tired of feeling it and tired of all the work it took to deal with. It was like my dog had lost control of his bowel and he was crapping all over the house. *Of course, I love you dog. Of course, I'll clean it up. But you're killing me here!* And like those piles of imaginary poop, shame was wearing me out. I wanted shame to stop. There had to be another way.

Victor Frankl brought me the missing piece. Frankl was an Austrian psychiatrist, a Holocaust survivor who chronicled his death camp experiences in his groundbreaking book, *Man's Search for Meaning*. Frankl saw the extremes of humanity. He saw the ugly and saintly ways human beings treated each other. Witnessing so much suffering, he realized that if there is to be any meaning in life, there must be meaning in suffering. Frankl wrote, "... suffering ceases to be suffering at the moment it finds meaning."

I was humbled and inspired by Frankl's experiences. Shame was causing me to suffer. This was the piece I'd been looking for: How to stop suffering. To make the shame stop, find its meaning.

Only You Can Heal Yourself

The time for someone else to make you feel loved and cared for is over. That was supposed to happen when you were a child. If it didn't, my heart goes out to you; sorry, that ship has sailed. Now the responsibility is yours – not your spouse's, family's, children's, friends', colleagues', or lover's. You must take care of your feelings and make yourself feel loved, understood, and accepted. There is no law that requires anyone to unconditionally love, rescue or understand you.

You create your feelings and that means you have the power to change them. Only you can feel your feelings. And only you can heal yourself. No one can feel for you. No one can give all the attention you need to heal except you.

The three Basics form your base for moving through the Four Simple Questions. Taking them to heart will save you a lot of work and time. The Basics set you up for success in Chapter 3 - Feeling Your Feelings, the centerpiece of the Shame Hack. You want to change how you feel? A good place to start is with feeling your feelings.

Some stories will be shared throughout the book that come from my clients, who have used this system to help themselves. I appreciate their generosity and courage. This is G's story.

G: I Don't Apologize For Who I Am

I'd been taught, trained, to give every last bit of myself. That meant holding back my opinions, never being angry, sarcastic, or even pointedly honest. It also meant trying to be perfect and dimming my light so others could be comfortable. That's what would give me love—sparing others' feelings and receiving their approval. I somehow came to believe that love originated outside of myself.

Now that I know I am loved, I approach new relationships differently. When I choose to allow someone new to get close to me, it is because I am loving myself and gifting myself with the relationship. It is my choice and according to my own pace. I am not pressured about it by outside sources. I need others, but not in the same way I previously thought. I don't need them to feel loved.

At one point after I realized I was loved, I fell in love with myself. I basked in the newness of feeling loved. Then reality set in, and I had to realize I needed to consciously understand that I was loved. The feeling and knowledge had to be explicitly taught, and then it had to reach my heart. It seemed unfortunate to me that I had to work toward this realization when it seemed to come so "naturally" for others who may have had an easier family life or a childhood with more fulfilled emotional needs. But now I am okay with it. I am doing a balancing act of opening my heart and also protecting myself. Before, I was so bipolar about such things—either I gave too much or closed myself off completely. Now I tell myself not to force relationships to work. I need to accept people as they are and understand they must do the same for me. It doesn't matter that I stumble clumsily around new and changing relationships. My baseline, my foundation, is the love I have for myself and the love I inhabit, which no one can take away from me.

Now that I know I am loved, there is no rush to hide my flaws, quirks, or strengths in order to collect approval from others. I don't apologize for who I am. If love from others comes up short or I am disappointed in the way I am treated, I still love myself. So I'm less wary when approaching new relationships.

-G

Chapter 3 – Feel Your Feelings

I'm Japanese-American, but my parents rarely speak Japanese around the house (unless they don't want me to know what they're talking about). At family gatherings, I hear my parents speak Japanese to my grandparents, and the only word I understand from their conversation is my name.

One of my college's graduation requirements was one year of a foreign language. I thought this was my chance to learn to speak Japanese. Since I'd heard Japanese all my life, I would be a natural.

Nope. On the first day of class, I learned instantly that a lifetime of hearing Japanese doesn't make you a natural at all. I was as confused as the other students were when the teacher started speaking Japanese. This was one of many "brilliant ideas" that only worked in my mind.

# # #

The point is this: Sometimes something you think should come naturally just doesn't. This is the case with feelings. It may seem ridiculous that we're going to talk at length about what it means to feel your feelings. But it's important to understand what "feel your feelings" means. The Four Simple Questions are a feelings-driven process. That's why we are going break it down.

You may resist experiencing your feelings, especially the uncomfortable ones. Perhaps you've suppressed your feelings and you've lost touch with them. I did. It's okay to be resistant or even confused by your feelings. You may even get in your head when it comes to feeling. The aim is to be in your body. This chapter (and Chapter 4 - Nuts & Bolts) describes the perspective and the tools to use to get familiar with and identify your feelings.

The "feelings" topics covered in the rest of this chapter are:

- What "Feeling Your Feelings" *Is*
- What "Feeling Your Feelings" Is *Not*
- The "Building Block" Feelings: Sad, Hurt, Anger, Fear, and Shame (SHAFS)
- Emotional Honesty

What Feeling Your Feelings *Is*

What does it mean to actually *feel your feelings*? Simply put, it means to experience, sense, and observe the emotions present in your heart, gut, or body.

To feel your feelings means to experience the impact and physiological expression of your emotions. Feeling your feelings means to experience the drama playing out inside you. It means experiencing your feelings without rationalizing, distracting yourself, or interfering with the process. You feel your feelings as they are, without judgment. You tune into your emotions and pay attention. You turn your focus inward and concentrate.

You suffer from a broken heart, not a broken mind. The hurt lies in your heart not your mind. Therefore, do not *think* your feelings. Thinking your feelings does not equal feeling your feelings. Thinking about playing the guitar is not playing the guitar. You can think *about* your feelings. You can think about *why* you feel as you do. But thinking does not touch your hurting heart. <u>You must feel to heal.</u>

Feeling your feelings is an act of self-love. It communicates to your heart tolerance and acceptance, and the value you place on it. It demonstrates that you are willing to walk your talk, and feel what your heart feels, that you're willing to feel whatever it takes to understand what your heart experiences.

Enduring your suffering proves you're a worthy cause. This is how you love yourself. This is how you give yourself the attention you need. Your willingness to suffer resonates with your heart in a meaningful way. Intentionally feeling your suffering provides the framework for feeling understood.

Heartfelt self-love includes demonstrating maturity, understanding, and compassion for yourself. You demonstrate maturity by taking time to understand your feelings and their impact. You empathize with your heart, showing you understand it. Your compassion is reflected in your attitude of acceptance.

Self-love is paying as much attention as needed. It means feeling what needs to be felt. It means refusing to abuse yourself. You refrain from taking out aggression or shame on yourself.

Self-love is *not:* a shopping spree, a day at the spa, a piece of chocolate, consuming intoxicants, or gorging on sugar. These are acts of self-indulgence - maybe even, in excess, self-destruction. Self-love is not invalidating how you feel. Together these acts may distract or stimulate you, but they don't heal you. They don't touch your heart. They never get to the root of the problem: How you feel deep down inside.

What Feeling Your Feelings Is *Not*

Sometimes it helps to understand something by clarifying what it is *not*. Here are some examples of what feeling is not:

Wallowing. Wallowing is rolling around in your feelings with a "woe-is-me" self-pity attitude. Feeling is moving through your feelings; wallowing is stagnation.

Rationalizing. Rationalizing is the sour grapes of feeling (for example, saying to yourself, *I didn't want to play, anyway* to cover the disappointment of not being picked to play on a team). Rationalizing can also be an intellectual understanding of your feelings: I feel this way because of "such and such." Logically explaining away your feelings is not feeling. Feeling is taking a blow on the chin and experiencing the full expression of the emotion; rationalization is never stepping into the ring and trying to win on a technicality. Rationalizing is explaining away your feelings.

Vacating. Vacating is spacing out, neglecting, or mentally running away from your feelings; feeling is staying put and taking ownership of how you feel.

Downplaying. Downplaying is discounting your feelings; feeling is honoring your experience.

Labeling. Labeling is putting a name on your feelings; feeling is what goes into earning the label. In other words, feeling is the heartbreak, tears, and longing you experience, not just saying you feel sad.

Carrying On. Carrying on is endlessly *talking* about how you feel; feeling is *experiencing* how you feel.

Rehashing. An interaction bothers you and you have feelings about it. Instead of feeling them, you rehash the scene in your mind over and over. You dwell on it. You ruminate. Your mind revs up because you are bothered. You repeatedly replay and analyze the scene in order to help you avoid your bothersome feelings.

What feelings are *not* are all the ways you avoid feeling. These acts take you out of your heart. To feel, you must be present with your heart, and nowhere else.

Sad, Hurt, Anger, Fear and Shame (SHAFS)

Spoiler alert: We are not going to be dealing with good feelings. Generally, good feelings aren't a problem. Good feelings are what *you want to feel.*

Shame Hack aims to help you identity and deal with five (and let's just say it, unpleasant) emotions: Sad, Hurt, Anger, Fear, and Shame. These are the "building block" feelings. The acronym SHAFS will help you remember them.

Learning to identify your feelings is like the old game show, Name that Tune. When you start, you may need to hear an entire song a few times before you can name it. But with more exposure to the song, you begin to recognize it more quickly. You become so familiar with it, you can "name that tune" within the first few notes. The same applies to identifying your feelings. The more you feel them, the easier it will be to identify them.

Let's talk about what each of the building block feelings feels like.

Sad feels like you want to cry. You feel melancholy. You feel down. You may notice sighing, heaviness on the chest, heartache, craving love or affection, shallow breathing, pain in the pit of your stomach, a feeling of emptiness, a feeling of longing, quivering breath, heaviness of spirit, a feeling of being weighed down, a feeling of the loss of strength, general muscle weakness, feeling choked up, watery eyes.

Hurt feels like your heart saying *ouch*. It's emotional pain. There's an injury or insult to your heart or ego. You may notice heart constriction, head throbbing, mind going blank, pain in the chest, sour stomach, loss of appetite, cramping of large intestine, nervous system "on alert." You want to cry.

Anger feels explosive. You may feel like you want to break or destroy something. You feel activated. You want to take action. You may feel like you want to punch someone in the face. You may notice clenched teeth, fists, raised blood pressure, raised heart rate, heart pumping harder, body heating up, eyes widening or narrowing, acute focus, inflated chest, breath holding, crying, hair standing up, feeling like you're on the verge of snapping, just snapped, a surge of hostile energy, loss of patience, muscle tension.

Fear feels like you are scared. There's anxiety. You're nervous. You're unsure. You're apprehensive. You may notice your face and neck flushing, dry mouth, queasy stomach, muscles under your scalp contracting, jaw clenching. You may feel frozen. Your mind stalls. You can't think. Your palms sweat. Your body perspires.

Shame is different than the other feelings. It is a feeling we identify with. That is, you don't *feel* bad, you *are* bad. You feel less-than. Somehow, you just don't measure up. You feel unlovable, that there's something wrong with you.

You may notice eyelids drooping, shoulders slumping, downcast eyes, avoiding eye contact, tuning out, heart pumping harder, foreign sensations on skin (disconnect from skin), inner shrinking, light numb tingling in body, hair on scalp standing up, face paling, blood pressure dropping, tear ducts activating, heart compressing, shallow breathing, half of your heart beating harder than the other, abdominal muscles contracting and staying that way, jaw drooping, intestines twisting, skin cooling, perspiring, shoulders elevating and head ducking.

Emotional Honesty

When I was a kid, my grandma enjoyed going to Las Vegas to play slots. This was her fun time. When she'd come home, I'd ask her, "Grandma, how'd you do in Vegas?" She would say, "I won $200," or "I won $80." Or "Not so good this time." What I never heard her say was: "Dolan, I lost $500, but won $200." I never got the whole truth. While this level of honesty is perfectly fine for entertaining your curious grandson, it's not perfectly fine for answering the Four Simple Questions.

When you answer the Four Simple Questions, you want the plain honest truth. You need to be emotionally honest with yourself. But what does that mean?

It's simple. Call it like you see it. Tell it like it is. If you feel sad, then admit you feel sad. If your feelings got hurt, then admit your feelings got hurt. If you feel shame, admit you feel shame. There's no one to impress and no one to cast judgments. It's just you and your feeling, so no need for deception.

Emotional honesty allows you to take your feelings seriously. There's no need to downplay how you feel. No need to make light or joke. No need to discount or invalidate how you feel. When you accept *what you feel* without conditions, you accept *yourself* without conditions.

Dishonesty

Being dishonest ensures your suffering. Why? When you pretend things are okay when they're really not, you leave that hurting part of you alone in the dark. The hurt never gets addressed, leaving you suffering and neglected. You put on your, *There's no need to do anything because everything is fine* face. But in actuality, you're dying inside.

When you are dishonest, you can't trust yourself. Why should you? You're being inauthentic. You're being fake.

When you finally take a step back from dishonesty, you may find yourself asking: What is the long game here? Where is your dishonesty supposed to take you, anyway? Is that somewhere you even want to go? How does your emotional dishonesty serve you?

Feeling Sadness

A while back, my friend Mikey and I went out for Pho (Vietnamese noodle soup) for dinner. I usually order Pho with rare steak, but tonight I ordered it with brisket. I'm in the mood for something gristly. Mikey ordered Pho with chicken, and we got to talking.

I talked about struggling to write this book. Mikey talked about the turbulence in his relationship with his girlfriend, Isabella. Two weeks before, they had moved in together. Mikey and Isabella have both had their struggles with substance abuse. Both of them have been sober for years now. I always admire Mikey's candor when it comes to his addiction. He speaks honestly and from the heart.

Mikey told me that he and Isabella went to the rodeo the previous Sunday. Mikey's friend, Vincent, was selling insurance at a booth, and Mikey wanted Isabella to meet Vincent and his fiancée, Cynthia. They were enjoying themselves until they got to the booth, when Isabella grew quiet and withdrawn. After an introduction and a chat, Mikey and Isabella walked off to check out the rest of the rodeo.

After a few minutes of silence, Isabella finally spoke. "You never told me Cynthia was so pretty."

Mikey was surprised. "Should I have?"

"Well, you could've said something."

"Look, I'm into you. I don't care what my friend's girl looks like. I love you. My friend's girl could be smoking hot or they could be butt ugly. I don't care. It doesn't matter to me. I love *you*. What do you want me to say? 'We are going to meet Vincent and Cynthia today and by the way, Cynthia is smoking hot!' Come on!"

Isabella responded with a dirty look. Mikey was left in a state of confusion. He didn't feel he'd done anything wrong. He didn't do something he wasn't supposed to do. But he was on the receiving end of some crap.

I took in Mikey's story. I asked him if he wanted my opinion. He said he did. My two cents was that Cynthia's looks may have triggered shame in Isabella. Perhaps Isabella suddenly wasn't "pretty enough." Anytime you're "not enough," it stings - if it doesn't downright hurt.

Then I did my "thinking-feeling thing" and came up with some potential truths for Isabella. Maybe Isabella doesn't know she's beautiful, or loved, or lovable. Or maybe she doesn't know she's safe. I shared these possible truths with Mikey.

I asked, "What do you think of the feedback?"

"I don't know. I mean I don't know what goes on inside Isabella's head."

"I know. Only she knows. I wonder if she's open to figuring out her truth?" In my mind, I was asking: *Don't you want to relate and understand her? Her truth could bring her some peace. You love this woman. You care about her.*

"It's not my job," he replied. My heart sank. I get it. That's true. It isn't Mikey's job to figure out what's going on in Isabella's head or heart. I understand. But I feel sad about it anyway. *What's up with that?*

I wonder what this sadness is all about. I start rolling it around. *Why am I sad? Hmm. The situation between*

Mikey and Isabella has no direct effect on me. But I still feel sad. I ask myself the Four Simple Questions.

I already know the answer to Question 1: What Am I Feeling? I feel sad.

Question 2: What Did I Make That Mean? I'm not immediately sure. I ask myself, *what did I lose here? Why the sense of loss?* I focus inside and feel. I believe there's a lost opportunity for connection, closeness, and intimacy. I want those things. I'm missing those things in my life at the moment. I feel the loss of those things. Okay, I got it. I make it mean there's a loss of connection.

I'm familiar with the Four Simple Questions, so I skip past the setup statements for Question 3 (What Does That Say about Me?), and get to the final statement. (All of the statements are covered in Chapter 15) I ask myself: *What do I need to know? Where's the hurt?* I go toward the pain. *Do I need to know I am connected?* No, that doesn't resonate. *Do I need to know I am intimate?* No. *Do I need to know I value intimacy? No, but I do. Hmm, what do I need to know?* I feel again. *What do I need to know? I am relatable?* Maybe. "Relatable" does twinge at my heart since the sadness was not that strong from the get-go. I don't anticipate a tearful breakthrough. I'm just not feeling it that strong.

Yes, something like relatable. *Do I not feel related to?* Yes, this is true. *So what do I need to know? I relate?* Sting! That's it. I relate. Yep, that's it.

I feel sad because I relate. I feel sad that I don't feel related to. I see how I project myself into Isabella's experience. I often emotionally insert myself into other people's experiences. It's how I relate. It's what I do. I want to feel what they feel. I want to understand what they feel. I want to understand where their feelings are coming from. I relate. I also want someone to do this with me. This truth is in line with my history. Got it. It's true. I do relate.

Last question: *What's the Truth?* I relate. Yep, umm-hmm, that's right.

Chapter 4 – Nuts & Bolts: How to Feel Your Feelings

When I was in my early 20's, I made plans to take my first snowboarding trip. The night before I left, I visited my buddy, Junior, to borrow his snowboard.

"Junior, you got any tips for me for tomorrow?" I asked.

Junior cocked his head at me. "Tips, like what?"

"Like how to snowboard. How do you do it?"

"I don't know. It's kinda like a combo of surfing and skating."

"Well, I don't surf."

"You have to do this heel-toe thing. You feel where your edge is."

"What's the heel-toe thing? What are you talking about?"

"You'll figure it out. You'll understand once you start."

"Why can't you just tell me?"

"Dude, you'll figure it out. Here, take the board. Have fun."

I wanted Junior to tell me specifically how to snowboard. A big ask, I know. Snowboarding isn't something you learn through a conversation like a new travel destination.

But once I started snowboarding, I began to understand just what Junior was talking about. I needed a little context and experience before I understood.

The same holds true for learning to feel your feelings. Once you start working the exercises and getting familiar with your feelings, you'll have the experience needed to understand what feeling your feelings means. You'll get a natural sense for how to feel your feelings, just as I got a feel for how to snowboard.

Now that you have a better idea of what "feel your feeling" means, let's talk about the nuts and bolts: How to actually feel your feelings. The following exercises will help you do just that.

Feeling Awareness

The first thing you want to do in developing feeling awareness is to become aware of what you do to *avoid* your feelings. Feeling-avoidance habits are often unconscious; you become so used to them you don't know you're doing them. But these habits are your first clue that you are having feelings. This is why you want to identify your avoidance habits.

In Exercise 1, Feeling-Avoidance Habits, circle all the behaviors that you engage in (or think you engage in). Fess up. Admit it. It's just you and the exercise. Be honest: Don't let anything slide.

What do *you* do? Do you become aggressive? Yes? Aggressive is a 'no' for me. I'm more a grandiose kind of guy. Instead of feeling, sometimes I gorge myself on my delusions of grandeur. Yum. This is way more me. Make your way through the habit list. What do you or don't you do?

I'll go first. Here are the habits I use to avoid feeling my feelings: I do a little retail therapy (shopping) every now and again. Retail therapy gets expensive and sure doesn't last long. I'm definitely guilty of immature behaviors. I can get passive-aggressive and go tit for tat. In fact, I do passive-aggressive the most. I'm also down for playing the blame game here and there.

I've been impulsive. I was really impulsive when my dad got sick. I was on edge and emotionally all over the place. When I was at the store I would buy all kinds of stuff I didn't need. I started grabbing bags of candy at the check-out aisle. I have learned that when I'm impulsive, it means I'm overdue for some grounding.

I also like to start projects. Yay! Projects are fun and so, so distracting. A new project gives me something else to think about. Maybe I start a deep house cleaning. Or I start to research a gadget I have no intention of buying, like a new camera. Or I start a knitting project. A friend of mine likes to start home improvement projects. Whatever it is, I'm trying to make myself feel better by being "productive."

These are the main habits I use to avoid feeling. When I find myself using my avoidance habits, I know it's time to check in. Something is bothering me that I need to look at.

Circle all the behaviors that apply, or write them on a separate piece of paper.

Exercise 1: Feeling-Avoidance Habits

Circle all that apply to you.

- Defensive Behaviors: yelling, being aggressive, domineering, righteous, explaining, justifying, talking down, acting "better than you," exhibiting hubris or grandiosity, needing to be right, needing to win, jealousy, exhibitionism
- Addictive Behaviors: drinking or drugging, gambling, shopping, cleaning, eating, smoking,

having compulsive sex, gaming, shopping, social media, working

- Immature Behaviors: pouting, giving the cold shoulder, throwing tantrums, pulling attitudes, being passive-aggressive, giving tit for tat, getting revenge, blaming, mean teasing, bullying, stonewalling, holding a grudge
- Rationalizing Behaviors: denying, downplaying, making something "okay" in your mind, explaining away
- Self-harm Behaviors: self-mutilating, scratching, cutting, burning, starving, binging and purging
- Risky Behaviors: thrill seeking, excitement seeking, impulsivity
- Miscellaneous Behaviors: starting new projects, constantly seeking to be the center of attention, creating drama, creating chaos, shutting down, playing with your phone

Your avoidance habits are indicators that something may be bothering you, too. Sometimes you get so busy with life you don't realize something is bothering you. When you learn your avoidance habits, you can recognize them when they pop up and know it's a sign to stop and reflect. Take a few moments to check in and ask: Am I avoiding something? Am I having feelings? Is something bothering me? Then pause, breathe, and feel.

Don't forget what feelings are *not*. Let's say you've caught yourself in a feeling avoiding habit. You realize you're having feelings. You check in with yourself. You breathe. You feel. Then nothing. Bzzzzt! You've come all this way and you're still not feeling. Why is that? Maybe you are doing one of the things listed below. Let's check:

What Feeling Is *Not* (circle all that apply):

- Wallowing
- Rationalizing
- Vacating
- Downplaying
- Labeling
- Carrying on
- Rehashing

Where's Your Focus?

Your feelings are all about *you*. They're your creation. They come from you. That's why the focus needs to be inside you. You are the one reacting.

Focusing inside directs your attention to what is within your power.

The next exercise is simple but valuable. When your thoughts and attention are directed outward, your energy is expended on things outside your control. Trying to change the world around you to suit your feelings better is often futile and frustrating. Instead, focus on what is in your power: How you feel. How you react. You do this by directing your attention inside you.

Exercise 2: Inside or Outside

To complete this exercise, put an "X" under the Outside or Inside column for each question or phrase.

Outside	vs.	Inside
	Why would they?	
	Why do I?	
	What am I?	
	Why can't they?	
	Why does he?	
	You need to …	
	If she ___, I'm going to ___	
	Why does this always happen to me?	

The answers follow.

ANSWERS Exercise 2: Inside or Outside

Outside	vs.	Inside
X	Why would they?	
	Why do I?	X
	What am I?	X
X	Why can't they?	
X	Why does he?	
X	You need to …	
X	If she ___, I'm going to ___	
X	Why does this always happen to me?	X

Head or Heart

When it comes to feelings, you're in one of two places: your head or your heart. Your head is where thoughts, mental chatter, and your inner critic live. Your heart space is where feelings begin, take root, and live.

"Head or Heart" is similar to "Inside or Outside." Put an X in the column that applies.

For example, the first item is "tears." When you experience tears, where are you? Your head or your heart? You are in your heart. Your heart feels sad and you are crying. The next item is "why?" When you find yourself focusing on the "why," you are in your head. You are trying to find reasons instead of feeling your feelings.

This exercise should give you a better awareness of when you are in your head vs. heart. Remember: You need to be in your heart to feel, not your head. If you are trying to access your feelings and find that you're doing things that are in the head column, stop and move your attention to your heart.

Exercise 3: Head or Heart?

Head	vs.	Heart
	Tears	
	Why?	
	I/you don't understand	
	Breathe	
	Revenge	
	Fight	
	Blame	
	Talking	
	Pulse	
	Gut wrench	
	Think	
	Feel	

The answers follow.

ANSWERS: Exercise 3: Head or Heart?

Head	vs.	Heart
	Tears	X
X	Why?	
X	I/you don't understand	
	Breathe	X
X	Revenge	
X	Fight	
X	Blame	
X	Talking	
	Pulse	X
	Gut wrench	X
X	Think	
	Feel	X

Feeling Breath

I live in San Diego, a beach town. When you spend time at the beach, you often see surfers standing and watching for the lull that comes between sets (a group of waves). They time their charge for the lull because it is easier to paddle out past the surf then. A Feeling Breath is a way of timing a lull inside you to help you feel. A Feeling Breath takes advantage of the lull in your respiration cycle. In that lull, in that calm, it's the easiest time to feel.

A diagram of a normal breath follows. There's an inhale that peaks, followed by an exhale. The exhale bottoms out, and then the next inhale begins. This is a normal breath. The inhale and exhale are smooth curved lines that mirror each other. Nice, easy, normal.

With a Feeling Breath, the inhale is faster and deeper than a normal inhale. The inhale leads to a sharp peak, synonymous with taking a deep breath. Then the exhale is slower than normal. When the exhale hits bottom, it flattens out. It is this moment, this lull in the breath when you are quiet and still. The lull after the exhale, and before the inhale, is when you want to feel. The lull is when you concentrate on what you're feeling.

NORMAL BREATH

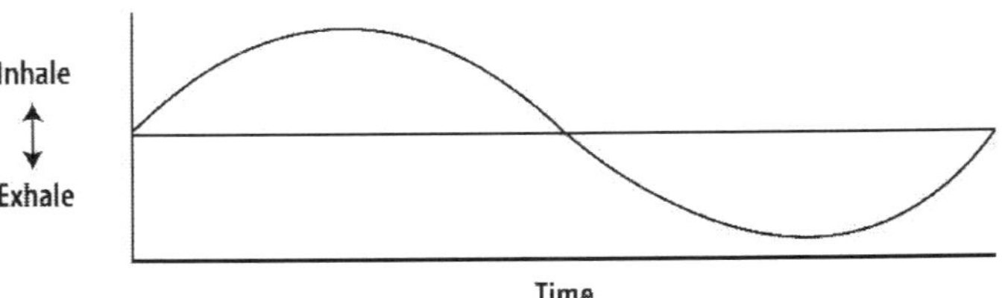

FEELING BREATH

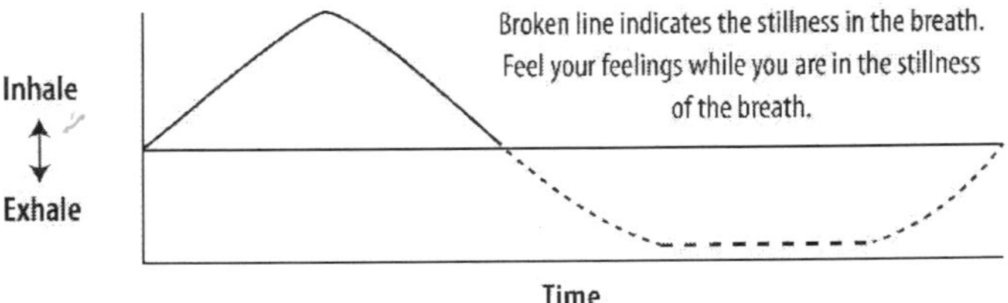

How to Do a Feeling Breath

Find a quiet place. Eliminate distractions. Clear your mind. Get comfortable. Take a few deep breaths to settle in. Close your eyes.

Take a deep inhale. Hold it for a moment, then release it slowly. As you start to feel almost all your air leave, focus attention on your feelings. Direct your attention inward. Hold your exhale a couple of moments and feel. Ask yourself: *What am I feeling? Am I feeling sad? Is that it*? Feel. Are you feeling sad? Identify your feeling.

Make your way through SHAFS one feeling at a time until you have identified your feeling. Begin with sad, then hurt, anger, fear, and finally shame.

You may need to try on a feeling, like you are trying on clothes, to see if the feeling fits. If you didn't identify your feeling on the first go-round, try a second round of feeling breaths. But this time, try on each feeling in the lull. Go through each feeling, one per breath.

Try doing a feeling breath now. Practice feeling in the lull.

Occupy the Mind

Sometimes when you struggle to feel, you just need to distract your mind a little. You may need to give your mind something to do while you feel. This is where Occupy the Mind comes into play.

Have you ever swum up to a beach ball in a swimming pool? You swim toward the beach ball but you can only get so close. You keep pursuing the ball but your wake keeps pushing it away. The only way to get the ball is to let it come to you.

This can happen when you are trying to feel your feelings too. One day, I was trying to feel my feelings but just couldn't do it. For some reason, I couldn't access what I was feeling.

When I get into a feeling mode, I'm like a pit bull with a cow bone. I go to town to feel my feelings. But I couldn't get there. I was tired. I needed a break from all my failed attempts. So, I sat up in bed and start playing Candy Crush on my tablet. I like playing mindless puzzle games. They occupy my mind. The game gives me something to focus on without requiring much thought.

As I played Candy Crush, my feelings started to rise. My eyes filled with tears. Suddenly, I found the sadness I'd been looking for. The sadness I wanted to let go. I continued to play until I felt the sadness set in. Then I put my tablet on the nightstand, grabbed a pillow, curled up on my side and let the sadness come out of me.

Like the beach ball in the pool, sometimes you have to let the feeling come to you. If you're actively pursuing a feeling and it's still not coming, take a break. Do something to occupy your mind. To occupy my mind, I've done chores. I've swept the house. I've vacuumed. I've listened to music.

Just do something that doesn't require a lot of thought. Any activity that gives you something to focus on but doesn't require much concentration.

Now it's time for the main event of feelings: shame.

Chapter 5 – Shamed to the Core

When I was 14 years old, my parents decided to repaint our house's interior. My dad was the DIY type. This means: *Dolan, cancel your weekend plans. It's family project time.* The walls hadn't been painted in years. They needed prep. I wiped them down and gave them a light sanding. Even though the walls were white, my dad wanted them primed.

I was priming in the living room when I noticed a splotch on the wall. The mark was about the size of a tangerine. I hadn't noticed the mark before, since it was hidden behind the couch. *What is that*? I took a closer look. *Oh, it's a water stain*. The mark was slightly darker than the surrounding white. I primed over it.

I finished priming the rest of the living room and returned to the water stain. It had bled through. I primed it again. *Maybe it needs a couple of coats*.

I moved on to priming the hallway. After finishing the hallway, I returned to the water stain. It had bled through again. I primed it again. *That should do it*. Nope. It came back the next morning.

I'll just paint over it. Primer isn't very thick. Paint should cover up the watermark. Coat one went on. Success? Nope.

The stain bled through. Coat two went on. Same result. Coat three went on. There it is again.

The paint dried in the living room and we moved the couch back. You couldn't see the stain anymore. Take that, water stain!

# # #

Shame Bleeds Through

Once, my therapist compassionately told me, "Dolan, you are shamed to the core." I never knew my condition had a name. I was taken aback she would've said such a thing. It felt like the truth; it hurt to hear. It seemed ominous. I didn't know what to make of this term. What did "shamed to the core" mean?

You won't find the name in the DSM-V, the medical book of mental disorders. And "shamed to the core" isn't a life sentence. But it is like that water stain: No matter how many times you cover it up, it keeps bleeding through. You can hide your shame. Or put it somewhere out of sight. But it's still there. If you want the water stain gone. You need to remove it and fill the hole. Which is what Shame Hack does to the shame staining your heart.

I didn't know my shame wasn't a life sentence until I learned to resolve it. With Shame Hack, the Four Simple Questions, and a willingness to feel, my attitude toward shame – and my experience of shame – evolved into something productive and meaningful.

What does "shamed to the core" feel like? It's not rainbows and unicorns; it's no one's daydream. Shamed to the core is like being one of the conjoined twins in *American Horror Story*. There's me and then there's my ugly, harsh, critical twin popping out of my neck. The cruel twin goes with me everywhere, like it or not. I can't get away. The shamed-to-the-core twin is always whispering in my ear: *You're not enough. You're lacking. You're a failure. What's wrong with you? Nobody cares*. He got his jollies making me feel worthless, undeserving and downright burdensome.

Being shamed to the core means you feel rotten inside. *I'm a bad apple, plain and simple. I lack redeeming qualities. I'm unworthy. There's nothing good about me.* Intellectually, I know this isn't necessarily true. But it *feels* that way. It's very convincing, especially if you feel things at a deep level. Shame ran so deep inside me, it hit my core being. This is who I am. I drank the shame Kool-Aid. I completely bought in.

That's the trouble with shame: it's so convincing. It *feels* so true. It can make you believe that down is up and up is down, that you're unlovable when you're not, that you're unacceptable when you're perfectly acceptable as you are, that there's always something to fear when you're actually safe.

The rest of this chapter focuses on my story. (I figure: fair is fair. If I'm going ask you to be honest and take a hard look at *your* shame, it only seems fair that I be honest too.) I'll show you how I've taken a hard look at my shame. I'll go first. I'll reveal my shame experience. So when it's your turn, you'll see there's nothing to be scared of. I'm not asking you to do anything I haven't done myself.

Back in the Day

I felt shame as a kid, though I didn't know that's what it was called. I felt "less-than," but back then I called it inferior. In school, I wasn't smart enough. I believed the smart kids were just born that way and I wasn't. In sports, I wasn't athletic enough. I wasn't the star athlete, the one to watch. I didn't do well with girls. I didn't feel attractive. I lacked confidence. And my lack of success only reinforced my belief that I was unlovable. The shame mantras played in my head continually.

I felt like I was out of place all the time. If I was at my friend's house, I should be home. If I were home, I'd rather be at my friend's house. I didn't feel I belonged.

Putting my finger on the exact causes of feeling shamed to the core is difficult. But I have come up with three: my sensitive nature, *bachi,* and my molestation.

First Cause: My Sensitive Nature

I'm a sensitive person. I was like that as a kid, too. Getting my feelings hurt was no fun. When you're shamed to the core, you get your feelings hurt all the time. The hurt seems to run deeper in you than other people. It doesn't take much of an offense to send a lightning strike to your core and get deeply hurt.

Being a sensitive kid was a curse. Now I see being sensitive as a blessing. It allows me to connect, empathize, and relate to people much more easily than an insensitive person can. Resolving shame in some of my dark and lonely places gives me the authenticity to connect with people in *their* dark and lonely places.

Paradoxically, shame's isolating nature creates an environment for genuine connection. You're alone in a dark place. Then someone joins you in your dark place. You can feel their presence. *Look, I have company. I'm not alone.* A connection is made, as if you were traveling in a foreign country and you hear someone speaking your native language. You connect with them. It's good to find someone who speaks your language. You can be the person who authentically relates to other people and speaks their language.

Second Cause: *Bachi*

I was raised in a culture of *bachi,* a Japanese concept that, as explained to me, means: *If you play with fire and get burned, you deserved it.* Raised with this mindset, when I felt shame I believed it was because I deserved it. This makes shame self-reinforcing. *I feel shame. I deserve it. I'm bad. So I should feel shame.* It made perfect sense to me. Shame hurt and felt like punishment.

But shame isn't punishment. It's just a feeling. People may try to punish you by shaming you. You can shame yourself as penance. But shame, in and of itself, is only a feeling. Just as happy, sad, joyful and sorrowful are neither punishments nor rewards. They're only feelings. They have their place. Shame does too.

Shame and honor were a big deal in my house. Bringing shame to the family was a big no-no. I didn't shame my family on purpose. I never intentionally set out to embarrass my parents. I was a hyperactive, curious boy who played and ran around. Sitting still for hours in a classroom was pure torture. This is how I remember it: I'm trying to sit still and behave. But it's like trying to stop an ocean wave from breaking. Impossible, I can't do it. I wiggle in my chair. Bounce my legs up and down. Talk to my neighbor. Try to have some fun, because I'm bored out of my bejesus. I'm an elementary school teacher's nightmare.

My behavior made for many unhappy parent-teacher conferences. My teachers informed my parents how "I disturb others and underperform." Then I'd hear about it at home and live in the shadow of parental disappointment.

I wasn't the pride and joy of my family and I knew it. I was the little troublemaker. I even had the "Here Comes Trouble" t-shirt to prove it. It was disheartening being the rotten apple of my parents' eye.

Third Cause: I Was Molested

Suffering sexual abuse as a child virtually guarantees you will feel shamed to the core. I've been there. My heart goes out to all survivors of sexual trauma. It's a dark and nasty experience.

There is nothing wrong with sharing something unfortunate that happened to you, in spite of what you may have believed (or been told). In fact, "telling" is generally the beginning of healing. My grandparents rarely spoke of their internment during World War II. They didn't do anything wrong and keeping silent didn't right that wrong. Silence provides cover for an unjust act.

Acknowledging the experience and its effects may help you move forward, but it is usually painful; talking about it can make the experience more real. I hope that writing about my experience will make it easier for you to talk about yours.

Sexual abuse is a serious problem. Catherine Townsend, in her 2013 study *Estimating a Child Sexual Abuse Prevalence Rate for Practitioners: A Review of Child Sexual Abuse Prevalence Studies*, found that one in 10 children will be abused before the age of 18. If you are the one in 10, know that you are not alone.

A word of caution: Shame Hack is not meant to help resolve trauma. If you experienced sexual abuse (either as a child or as an adult) within your family system; repeatedly over weeks, months, or years; that was violent; or if you are experiencing flashbacks about the abuse; or if you are experiencing debilitating anxiety or panic attacks in similar environments or with particular people, make Shame Hack your *second* step. For your first step, take loving care of yourself by working through the trauma with a qualified professional. Then come back to Shame Hack and lovingly attend to the residual shame.

As you begin to talk about your abuse, you may find that some people speak out against you, blame you, deny your reality, or judge you. For this reason, when you first share your experience, make sure you share it with someone safe – someone who will honor and hear you, who will be understanding and show compassion. Maybe someday those detractors will come around. Maybe not. Either way, it's not up to you or me. What is up to us is the decision to share. Perhaps someday, when you are ready, you will talk about your experience and someone else will find it easier to begin their healing journey. Your light will illuminate another survivor's dark place.

# # #

I grew up in the Southern California suburbs, a middle-class community of tract homes in a good school district. I don't remember exactly how old I was when I was molested. I think it happened around first grade, when I was six years old. The abuse was a one-time event perpetrated by a teenage neighborhood kid. I didn't know him well.

This is my memory:

It's a warm spring afternoon. I'm alone, playing on the side of my house where some bushes and hedges make a natural fort. The four-foot-high hedges block the view from the street but allow me to see out. I revel in the seclusion. I pretend my fort is a secret army base. Johnny, a lanky teen with feathered blond hair comes rolling down the street on his chrome BMX bike. I come out from behind the hedges and walk over to the sidewalk, hoping he might play with me.

"Hey, Johnny, where you going?"

"I'm going over to Ernie's."

"What are you going to do over there?"

"Give him some candy."

At this age, I'm a candy fiend. It's my weakness. "I want some candy!"

"Ok, come back here and I'll give you some." Johnny walks his bike over to the hedges. I follow. Johnny takes a seat in the grass behind the bushes. I sit next to him. "I'll give you some candy if you do something for me."

"Ok, what?"

With his pointer finger, he signals me to lean in. He whispers, "I want you to give me a blowjob."

I have no idea what he's talking about. I just look at him, blank-eyed. He pulls down his pants. Out pops "Mr. Worm."

"Lick it like a lollipop." He holds the base of Mr. Worm.

Eww, that's where pee comes out, *I think as he starts playing with himself to get hard.*

"I'll give you candy after you lick it."

I lean over and put my head in his crotch. I feel his humidity on my face. Brown hair pokes up like a pubic hair loofah. White boxers with a green diamond pattern hug his thighs. I put my tongue out and dab Mr. Worm like I'm licking the top of a 9-volt battery. Yuck, it tastes salty. Liar. This doesn't taste like a lollipop!

"Lick it again."

I'm apprehensive. I don't like the taste or the smell. I'm dabbing at it. In no time, Johnny gets frustrated.

"I want you to do it like this."

Johnny slides my pants down. He leans over and puts his mouth around my penis, which is hairless, like a newborn hamster. This is the weirdest sensation. His mouth is warm and moist. I feel so strange. My penis wants to retreat into my stomach, like a startled tortoise head. My penis feels so strange I wish I could detach it. My skin crawls. Overwhelmed by a rush of foreign sensation, I squirm. My stomach turns. He carries on for a few moments.

I don't know what to make of this. Johnny is making me feel like I have to pee. My testicles are starting to feel like what my foot does when it falls asleep. This is all so strange. Johnny stops. I pull my pants up.

"Do it like that."

I lean in and try again, still apprehensive. I don't want to reverse Golden-Rule this one. I don't want to do unto him what he just did unto me.

Johnny is still frustrated. He's still not getting what he wants. He pulls up his pants, tosses me the candy, and rides off. I never encounter him again.

I feel strange, queasy and tingly at the same time. If my body is a temple, it just got overrun with ants. Ants everywhere.

I've done bad. I know I'm not supposed to pull my pants down in front of anybody. And my parents don't want me to eat candy. I'm scared I'll get in trouble. I better keep this to myself.

# # #

Looking back, I see that my life seemed to get more difficult after I was molested. I was more hyperactive. I wet the bed. I wanted constant stimulation, physical or mental. I needed intense engagement. I desired undivided attention. Intense interaction was my refuge from feeling creepy in my body. The intensity focused me on the moment, a place outside of my body. This is how I dealt with the discomfort as a child. Hyperactivity was my sanctuary.

Being molested primed my sexual curiosity too early. Being sexually curious at such a young age is rare, and a natural consequence of sexual abuse. I'm curious by nature anyway, but being so curious about sex at age six is shaming. I became sexually precocious. I felt like a dirty, horny, pervert at age six, thinking: *Something is wrong with me. The other kids aren't like me. I must be bad. I am unacceptable. I have to keep who I am a secret.*

Sexual trauma can leave a black mold on your soul. The mold pumps its toxic byproducts into your system long after the event is over. When the toxins hit your system, their exact effects on your mind, body and spirit become difficult to pinpoint. You're not feeling well; is it because of your mind, your body, your spirit, or a combination? While trauma's effects vary by individual, sexual trauma survivors almost inevitably feel shame to the core.

We are going to continue looking at shame in the next chapters and I've got some good news: it's going to be okay.

Journaling Exercise:

Answer the following questions:

1. What was your experience of belonging as a child?
2. How did you experience shame as a child?
3. What did your family consider shameful?
4. What did your family teach you about shame?
5. What is your earliest memory of experiencing shame?
6. If you experienced sexual trauma as a child, how has it affected you?

Chapter 6 – The Hotel on the Cliff

In the summer, when the coastal ocean temperature climbs above 65 degrees, I like to swim in La Jolla Cove. I meet up with friends and we swim from the cove to La Jolla Shores and back, about two miles round trip. I've made this open water swim many times. But, every time I do, I'm anxious until we start heading back. When I lift my head out of the water and see the hotel on the cliff, I know everything is going to be okay. I finally relax.

Sometimes you have to see a path to safety before you can relax. When I learned how to resolve shame, I saw a path to safety. I knew it was going to be okay. I could relax.

Feeling Your Feelings Isn't Enough

I used every tool at my disposal on my search for an inner path to safety. I faithfully attended group therapy three times a month for months. I had individual sessions once a quarter. I'd check in with my "group buddy" daily to practice connection and intimacy. I wrote letters and read them aloud in group to complete open-ended relationships.

I kept working to get to the bottom of my shame. The weeks turned into months, and the months into years. This wasn't easy for me. I'm not a big fan of vulnerability – the emotional nakedness necessary to feeling my own shame, to owning how unworthy I felt. I wondered: *Where does shame end?* The benefits of feeling my feelings had plateaued. Simply feeling my feelings wasn't working any more. Feeling my feelings had taken me from cluelessness to awareness and to accurately identifying my feelings. Feeling my feelings had also taken away my fear of feeling and gotten me used to experiencing them, which was a great improvement. However, I needed something to make the shame stop. But at the time, I didn't even know that was possible. Shame seemed like a life sentence.

Shame in My DNA

I'm in private practice. Whenever I take a class from my chiropractic mentor, he quotes research from a variety of sources: science, medicine, Eastern thought, philosophy, and so on. In a recent class, he gave me some of the books he cited. One is about metaphysics. Its author argues that even single-celled organisms have some form of consciousness.

This passage got me thinking. *Hmm. I wonder if I can feel shame at a cellular level?* I put the book down and closed the windows. I turned down the lights. I lay down in bed. I became as still as possible. I quieted my mind and focused on my breath. I felt as deeply as I could.

Surprise! There it is. I feel shame down to my cells. *Oh shit! Even my cells have shame. WTF?! I'm screwed. I'll never get away. There's no escape.*

I was disturbed.

I gathered myself. *I wonder if I can feel shame in the nucleus of the cell. Does shame go even deeper*? I calmed myself and start to feel again. Then *BOOM*, there it was *Shame is in my DNA. I can't believe it. All the way down to my DNA, really*?

Discovering shame in my DNA intrigued me. *Shame is in my DNA. Huh. What does that mean*? *If shame is in my DNA, it means that I have no control over it*. Then epiphany struck. *If shame is in my DNA, that means it's not my fault!*

It's not my fault that I feel shame. I have no control over it. Just like I have no control over my eye color, height, or skin color. It's not my fault I have brown eyes. It's not my fault I feel shame. It's in my DNA. I can't help it. I'm normal. Whew!

I had just turned my *bachi* indoctrination on its head. I don't feel shame because I *deserve* it. No, I feel shame *because it's in my DNA*.

The Way Out of the Chinese Handcuffs

This realization did a couple things. For one, it helped lift a big burden. I was relieved that there was nothing wrong with me, even if I felt shame. Shame was no longer a deep personal character flaw. Shame was a normal human feeling. The realization also helped stop the runaway shame train: feeling shame that I feel shame, then spiraling to a dark, isolated place. I was freed to think about shame differently.

Shame is tricky. Shame always wants me to be a little bit more because I am not enough. I realized that, instead of trying to get to the bottom of my shame and eliminate it once and for all, I needed to learn to resolve it - because it wasn't going away. I was trapped in it, just like the "Chinese handcuffs" I played with when I was a kid.

I think the real name was "Chinese finger trap." It was a cylinder of braided bamboo strips about six inches by one inch. You stick one finger in each end past your knuckles. Then, when you try to pull your fingers out, the woven bamboo clenches down. The harder you pull, the tighter the cylinder becomes, locking your fingers in the tube. The trick to escape is to do something counter-intuitive: Push your fingers together, further into the tube. This loosens the constriction around your fingers. Then, with the cylinder loose, you place your thumbs on the end, holding the tube inward and slide your fingers out to escape.

This was me with shame. I kept trying to pull away from shame, but it kept cinching down on me. I was trying to escape but I couldn't. I didn't know the trick. Yet.

Just as Chinese finger traps don't release your fingers when you pull away, shame was not about to release me when I pulled away.

During a three-day intensive personal growth seminar that I co-facilitated, I taught the "downward and upward feeling spirals" I had recently developed on my way to Shame Hack. At the time, all I had was these two diagrams. I didn't have any questions or process to resolve shame yet. But I was thrilled with the cycles nonetheless.

Here's a quick version of what I presented. In the downward spiral, you have feelings that cause you pain.

You repress what you feel, and then stagnate. Repression can range from preoccupation and rationalization to addiction, obsession, and suicide. Each turn of the cycle makes you less willing to feel your feelings. This downward spiral leads to a numb and meaningless life in which your motivation is stopping pain and seeking pleasure.

DOWNWARD SPIRAL

FEELING

PAIN

REPRESSION

STAGNATION

With every turn of the cycle you become less willing to feel and decrease in feeling awareness

Downward Spiral leads to a numb, meaningless life

MOTIVATED BY:
Stopping pain & seeking pleasure

Range: Preoccupation and rationalization ⟶ Addiction, obsession, and suicide

In the upward spiral feelings lead to meaning, which stops suffering and results in growth. And with each turn of the cycle you become more aware of and willing to feel your feelings. Feeling emotional pain and discomfort becomes less of a barrier. You are now motivated by thorough enjoyment. Take learning to play the piano as a simple example. Acquiring this knowledge will inevitably bring some discomfort. Your hands and back will tire and ache. There will be struggle, but frustration must be overcome. If your motivation was avoiding pain and seeking pleasure, you would quit at the first moment of discomfort. But if you are motivated by thorough enjoyment, discomfort is simply part of the process. The joy of playing the piano overrides the pain, discomfort, and struggle of learning to do it. The upward spiral leads to a rich, fulfilling, and meaningful life.

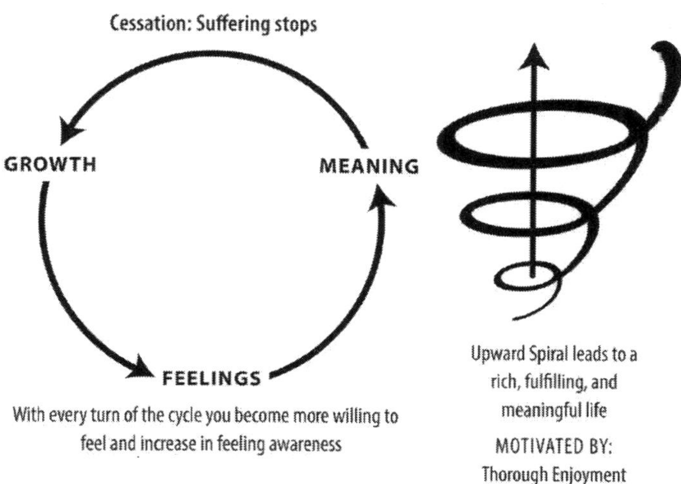

I drew the diagrams on the white board and enthusiastically explained them. The small, intimate audience of six looked at me, nodding their heads *Yes.* But that was it – no questions. Their reaction was, *That's interesting.*

What a disconnect. I had been really excited to share the cycles, and got a lukewarm reception. Where's the parade and marching band? To me, the diagrams were the answer to resolving painful feelings. They mapped out the path forward. In my mind I was showing them the fountain of youth, and they were saying, *Gee, that's a lovely fountain.*

I Find the Meaning

Two days later, I was at home reflecting on this experience. I was feeling sad that my diagrams were a flop. My sadness morphed into shame. I started to berate myself. *Dolan, why do you obsess about your feelings like this? What is wrong with you? Other people don't do this. You're such a loser. Why can't you just let it go? What's your problem? Why do you keep trying to fix yourself? You keep trying and trying. You fail every time. You're always trying something new. The problem is* you. *Give up already*!

I heard enough. I was sick and tired of feeling shame all the time. I wanted to try a different approach. I wanted to try to reframe the meaning of my shame. Victor Frankl's book, Man's Search for Meaning, came to mind. I started playing around with how to find the meaning in my feelings. For the first time, instead of just stewing in it and feeling it. I turned and faced my shame and wondered, *How do I find the meaning in my shame?* I started with a simple fill-in-the-blank statement: *The fact that I feel shame means* ______.

My impulse to identify with my shame kicked in. *It means you're a loser who can't figure it out*. No … think about it differently. Why would you keep trying new things to fix yourself? Why would you do that, Dolan?

I like to try new things. It's fun. I can't help it. I'm curious. That statement hits me: *I'm curious*. Suddenly, I'm overcome with emotion. I tear up. That's why I keep trying new things. Yes, lots of things I try fall flat. But I keep trying. I'm not hopeless. I enjoy novelty. I have a desire to understand. This is the meaning of my shame. I'm not feeling shame because I'm "a loser who can't figure it out." I'm feeling shame because I don't realize what it means to be curious, to embody a desire for novelty and understanding. I'm a curious person. This is who I am.

The shame lifts off me.

There's a reason *I am curious* made such an impact. As a kid growing up, I was curious. I would get into stuff. I would poke around. I was nosy. My curiosity got me in a lot of trouble. Consequently, I thought being curious was something bad, something shameful that needed to be suppressed.

When I was five years old, my family visited my grandma's house. I was in her bathroom. She was diabetic. She left her blood sugar testing machine on the bathroom counter. I'd never seen it before. A shiny plastic box with buttons, lights, and switches! I had to see what the mystery box did. I was by myself; no one could see me. I couldn't help myself. I started to push all the buttons and flip the switches. The box didn't do anything exciting. I left the bathroom. Hours later, I was confronted: Did you play with grandma's glucose testing machine? *How do they always know it's me?* I just stared at my dad, uncle, and grandma. Then they proceed to give me the business and tell me not to touch anything. Shame and curiosity are fused together inside me.

All these years, being curious was a source of trouble, something shameful, not acceptable. But when my shame took on a new meaning, hope was restored, acceptance embraced.

I had figured out how to find the meaning in my shame, and shame stopped. Eureka! Finally, at last, after all this time, shame went away. It's like rays of sunshine suddenly beamed through the thick clouds overhead and choral music resounded. *Is this happening? I can feel it. I can feel the difference. I don't feel shame anymore. Can I trust this? I'll have to try again and make sure this wasn't a fluke.* Sure enough, the next time I felt shame and ran it through the meaning statement, it stopped. Stopping shame was my hotel on the cliff. I got shame to stop twice in a row, and I knew it was going to be okay. I could do this.

Now I use the Four Simple Questions whenever I feel shame. As a result, the volume of my inner critic has clicked down. I'm replacing my inner critic with inner peace. Peace spreads across my inner landscape. My truth brings relief, peace and understanding.

Your truth will do the same for you. But don't take my word for it. Find out for yourself.

Journaling Exercise:

Answer the following questions

1. What is your "hotel on a cliff"? What do you need to see that would represent a path to safety?
2. What does your path to safety look like?
3. How do you react to the metaphor "shame in your DNA"? Is it disturbing? It is relieving? What is your experience?
4. What types of things does the voice of shame say to you?

Chapter 7 – From Painful to Meaningful

I felt shamed to the core for nearly four decades. I'm fertile ground for seeds of self-doubt. To uproot these weeds of doubt, I've had to learn many truths about myself over the years.

When you look at my truth list below, please appreciate that I felt the opposite of the truth. I lived *not* knowing the truth. I had to learn the truth for myself. For example, the truth, *I am safe*. I lived scared. I lived not knowing I'm safe.

Not knowing you are safe affects how you think and act. You live a vigilant life. You stay alert for impending doom. You walk around with your stomach tight. You crave certainty. You take rigid positions. You have more faith in words than people. Until you learn the truth *I am safe,* then you can relax. You can release your death grip.

Shame once made me believe I was unworthy. *I don't feel worthy. I live in a world of unworthy. I'm undeserving of good things. Unworthy of love.* I think, feel, and behave accordingly. This was my world until I learned the truth. *I am worthy*. Then my world changed. Love can make its way in, instead of being turned away at my wall. I can be proud of myself, and allow praise to sink in. Kindness can influence me for the better instead of making me suspicious. I am more available for deeper connection.

Not all the truths on the list are related to shame. Some truths came from other feelings, such as sad, hurt, anger, or fear. Some truths are more meaningful than others, such as: I am safe, I am determined, and I belong.

Here are some of the truths I've learned. I am …

Safe	Curious	Merciful
Worthy	Hopeful	Appreciative
Caring	Grateful	Determined
Deep	Healable	Forgiving
Free	Creation**	Trusting
Proud	Resilient	Responsible
Fragile	Conscious	Willful
Someone who belongs		Perfect
A student of the heart*		

* This is about being willing to learn what my heart has to teach me.

** This is a spiritual truth. I am part of the fabric of the Universe, not a just a patch on it.

A Whole New World

Your world can change with one truth. I've seen it happen. When someone learns the truth *I am safe*, their world changes. I tell them, "If you don't feel safe you don't have much. Don't be surprised if you start having more fun. It's hard to enjoy life when you're scared all the time." When you feel safe, you're not waiting for impending doom. You don't have to clench your stomach waiting for a punch to your gut. You can have a soft belly. You can relax and exhale. You can be yourself instead of a frightened version of yourself.

How Can This Be?

When you find the meaning in your shame, you are changing a core belief. Your beliefs, thoughts, and feelings connect in a cycle. Your beliefs create your thoughts. Your thoughts create your feelings. Your feelings reinforce your beliefs. And around it goes.

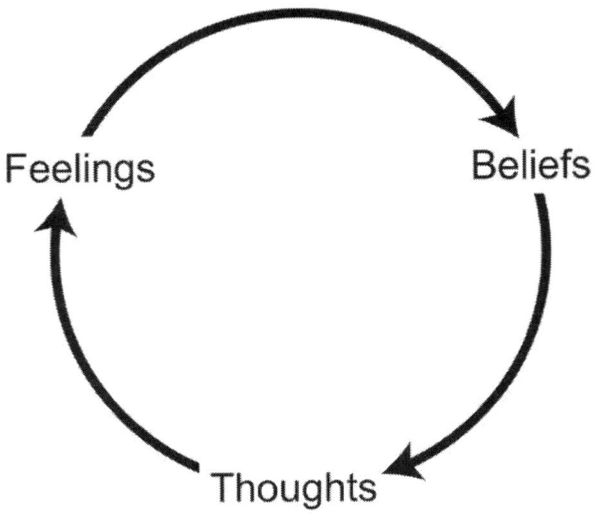

How do you change how you feel? By changing what you believe. Change what you believe and you change your thoughts. Change your thoughts and you change how you feel. This is what Shame Hack does. It helps you change what you believe about yourself, which leads to a change in how you feel.

This is what's great about Shame Hack. You only have to change your beliefs once to change how you feel from here on out. That's the beauty of it. You don't have to work on an issue over and over again.

What Happens When You Stop Feeling Shame?

The first thing you'll notice when you stop feeling shame is that the pain associated with shame stops. You feel relieved. You can breathe again.

One of the most common outcomes of resolving shame is that you feel more comfortable in your body. You feel more comfortable in your own skin. You feel more comfortable being *you*. The fear of shame decreases because you know who you are and how to deal with it successfully. Your confidence grows. You feel free. You have arrived.

Life is better when you are not shamed to the core. You feel more open, happier, secure, accepting and confident. You become available to experience relationships differently.

Finding your truth gives you a piece of your new identity. You get to know who you really are. Achieving your potential becomes more of a reality. What will you do with all the energy recovered from trying to protect yourself from shame? Where will you put your energy? You can invest your energy in passion instead of protection.

Feel to the Core

There's a hidden upside of feeling shame to the core. "Shamed to the core" implies that negative condition that you feel deep down. But it's the opposite. The shame you feel so deeply has a positive side: It means you have the capacity to *feel deeply*. In other words, shame to the core means you can feel to the core. The goal is to move away from shame and into something more enjoyable. If you feel shame to the core, then you can feel inspired to your core. Joy to the core. Love to the core.

Removing shame impacts you in many ways. If shame affects your close relationships, then removing shame can transform those relationships. If shame affects your confidence at work, then removing shame can boost your confidence at work. If shame affects your self-compassion, then removing shame can increase compassion for yourself and others. The more shame impacts your life, the more its removal will liberate you.

Think of all the situations, circumstances, and ways that shame has lied and made you feel not enough, unsafe, unlovable, unacceptable, that you don't belong. That there's something wrong with you. That you're the only one, and you can't do anything right. These are all the ways in which removing shame can liberate you. With shame, all you hear is your inner critic chirping. With shame removed, your inner critic falls silent.

The Four Simple Questions transform your experience of shame from painful to meaningful. Your willingness to feel your feelings lays out a path to feeling your purpose deep down. You have something positive to contribute that only you can give. You have something valuable to contribute buried underneath your shame. Grab a shovel. It's going to be okay.

Chapter 8 – Identifying Shame: The Crux of the Issue

In my last year of chiropractic school, I enrolled in a board review class to help me pass the final National Chiropractic Board Exam to get licensed.

At 8:00 a.m. on the first day, the instructor started his lecture.

"Three hundred seventy-five. Know this number." he said. "Three seventy-five is the bottom line. Three seventy-five is passing. Who can tell me what 376 is?"

The class sat in silence, not sure what he's asking.

"Three seventy-*six* is showing off!"

In the spirit of my instructor, identifying shame is your 375. Identifying shame is the crux of the issue. When you identify shame, you can resolve it. If you can't identify shame, you may believe shame's lies and get stuck.

Just for all you overachievers out there, know that 375 is enough. You don't need 376 or more. Three seventy-five is enough and so are you.

Shame Is a Barrier

Shame acts as a barrier to emotional healing. Robert Karen, in his book Becoming Attached, has this to say:

"Therapy can do many things. It can provide a new model of what a close relationship can be ... and it can offer a safe haven where feelings of shame no longer present such a terrible barrier to self-exploration ... shame is a critical barrier to the entire working through process."

Shame can stop you before you even get started. This is why it's important you identify shame. When you identify shame, it loses some of its power. You realize that shame is a feeling, like any other feeling. Shame is not the truth of who you are.

It's Not Your Fault

Shame is in your DNA. Shame is in everyone's DNA. Everyone feels it. Brene Brown writes, "Shame is universal – no one is exempt."

Shame is the product of evolution. You can't help that you feel shame. It's not your fault. There's nothing wrong with you. Shame is not punishment. It's just how you're wired, like walking upright. Shame serves an evolutionary function. It is considered a "self-conscious emotion," and like other self-conscious emotions, it is *"probably [an] evolved response to aid in solving recurrent problems associated with living and managing one's relationship to others."* (Lickel, Schmader, and Spanovich)

Shame can warp your mind into thinking *If I'm critical of myself – if I shame myself – then at least I can feel good about that. I'm conscientious enough to punish myself. I'm guilty of this.* If you do this too, there's a reason for it.

"Despite their differences, pride, shame, and guilt all activate similar neural circuits ... This explains why it can be so appealing to heap guilt and shame on ourselves – they're activating the brain's reward center." (Korb and Siegel)

It's not your fault you feel shame or shame yourself. There are reasons. While shame may be part of your makeup, you can take your power back by first learning to identify it.

We Identify With Shame

Shame is different from the other building block feelings: sad, hurt, anger, and fear. For example, when you feel sad, you are melancholy. You feel like you're going to cry. You recognize you feel sad.

But when you feel shame, you identify with it. You don't just *feel* bad. You *are* bad. You embody the feeling

When shame is strong, it's convincing. So much so you believe you're bad. You believe how shame feels.

Identifying with shame is what makes it so tricky. For example, you feel unlovable. You're not unlovable, you just *feel* that way. What you actually feel is shame. The truth is you are lovable. Period. You are lovable without conditions or special circumstances, or only with certain people. You just don't know it yet. You don't have visceral certainty. You don't know the truth.

Shame is all smoke and mirrors. You feel unworthy. You are not an unworthy person, though: What you feel is shame.

Here's another: You feel that you don't belong. You are not an "unbelonging" person. What you feel is shame. When you recognize what shame feels like, you can identify it and not buy in.

You feel shame when you identify with not being "enough." *I'm not smart enough* turns into your identity: *I'm stupid. I'm not skinny enough* morphs to *I'm fat. I'm not pretty enough* internalizes into *I'm ugly. I'm not successful enough* means *I'm a loser.* This is how shame feels.

The crux of the issue is: you must learn to recognize when you feel shame. When you recognize the feeling, you can work through it. You can do something about it. If you don't recognize it, you just sit in it feeling less-than, not enough, and *I'm the only one.*

Shame Indicators

To identify shame, you need to increase your awareness of shame. Increased awareness helps you detect it. Learning your shame indicators, shame triggers, and shame defenses will help get shame on your radar.

Shame indicators are the first clues that you may be feeling shame. Learn these indicators, and when you experience one, check in with yourself and see if you feel shame.

Circle the indicators that pertain to you:

- The first twinge of emotional pain inside
- When you feel like isolating
- When you feel like a "bad person"
- When you feel like retreating or you want to flee
- When you want secrecy
- When you feel scared of getting caught or exposed

- When you fear the judgment of others
- When you feel compelled to play an inauthentic role (such as successful, happily married, parent of a perfect family)
- When you feel like a fraud, or that you are living a lie
- When you feel jealousy or envy

The indicators help get shame on your radar. Recognize when you experience an indicator and check in to see if you feel shame. Remember: the goal is to become aware when you feel shame so you can do something about it.

Shame Triggers

You want to be thought of as a good person, not only by others but yourself too. What often triggers shame is the potential exposure of a perceived negative personal characteristic.

Triggers are characteristics that produce shame in you because you can't stand admitting that you have them. Triggers may reflect something you don't like about yourself.

Look at the "Shame Triggers" list. On a first pass, circle the characteristics that trigger shame for you - especially the ones you don't want anyone else to know about. Then go back and circle the characteristics that resonate for you in a strong and offensive way. Those are the characteristics that you can't stand in other people. These may be hidden sources of shame you push onto other people, so you don't have to acknowledge them in yourself.

Shame Triggers

Weak	Difficult	Manipulative	Can't feel/numb
Needy	Lazy	Deceitful	Never happy
Shy	Insecure	Narcissistic	Self-centered
Cheap	Greedy	Indecisive	Hot-tempered
Selfish	Violent	Unlovable	Lacks direction
Lost	Explosive	Annoying	Addict/Alcoholic
Sad	Sloppy	Impatient	Overbearing
Mean	Cheater	Fat/Thin	Self-absorbed
Cruel	Sadistic	Unsatisfied	Bad parent
Angry	Hopeless	Inferior	Hot-tempered
Loser	A burden	Irresponsible	Hypocrite
Stupid	Negative	Pessimistic	Can't figure it out
Slow	Scared	Deceptive	Low self-esteem
Dumb	Unhappy	Immature	Unforgivable
Gay	Bitter	Depressed	Untrustworthy
Quiet	Poor	Unacceptable	Not capable
Weak	Pathetic	Irritating	Criminal/Felon
Slutty	Hateful	Freeloader	Uses people
Rich	Racist	Virginity	Genitalia

Impossible to please   Damaged your child

Don't know who you are   Don't know what you want

What you feel shame about is personal. Are there any other personal negative flaws that don't appear on the Trigger list? Go ahead and add them.

The characteristics most difficult to admit are our biggest sources of shame. Here's what I mean: I can admit I'm immature. I know being immature is nothing to brag about, but admitting it doesn't bother me. I own it. Being immature means I will laugh at a fart joke. I will hold grudges for too long. I can act petty. All immature stuff. It's shameful. But I'm at peace with being immature. I accept that I'm immature. If someone called me immature, I wouldn't necessarily like it. But it wouldn't bother me much.

But admitting I'm selfish kills me. It triggers shame. I don't want to admit I'm selfish. If someone calls me selfish, it hurts. I don't want to think of myself like that. If I perceive other people as acting selfish, I want to judge them for it. I may push my shame onto them, so I don't have to feel it. I draw a distinction: *They are selfish, and I am not.* I take offense. *We are not the same. I would never be selfish like that.* Pushing your shame onto other people is something to be aware of. When you push your shame, it's likely you have a source of deep shame and pain that needs attention. That's why you circled characteristics that were strongly offensive.

The Shame Bucket

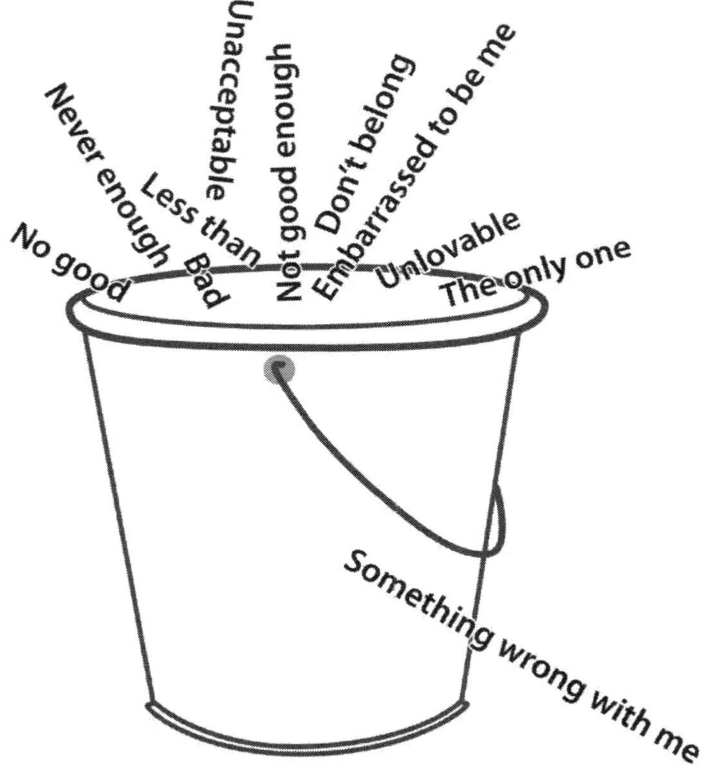

When you catch yourself feeling "less than," "not enough," "I'm the only one," – stop, and realize you feel shame. All these less-than feelings fall into the Shame Bucket.

How do you experience shame? Imagine you have consistent trouble passing a test. What do you feel when you discover your third attempt has also ended in failure? Do you feel like something is wrong with you? Do you feel not smart enough, less-than, the only one, or insignificant? Do you feel like nothing you do is ever good enough, or like you don't belong or fit in with others that had no trouble passing the test? These are some feelings that fall into the Shame Bucket.

When you feel unloved, unacceptable, invisible, unworthy, or any of these other "bad" things, what you feel is shame. Listing all of your shame characteristics when you are not feeling shame helps you identify them when you do feel shame.

Create your own Shame Bucket. Refer to it when trying to identify what you feel.

Shame Defenses

Now that you are increasing your awareness of shame, you need to identify how you defend yourself from feeling shame. The following is a list of common defenses to shame.

Circle the defenses that you use:

- Intimidate, dominate, or control others

- Blame others or make them the problem
- Acting out
- Playing the victim or attempting to win sympathy
- Withdrawing or ruminating
- Making yourself feel superior or becoming invulnerable
- Denying your emotional needs
- Caretaking or saving others
- Looking for someone to save you
- Exhibitionism
- Self-Harm
- Addiction

The point of identifying your defenses is not to add to your shame—as if you are doing something bad—but to increase your awareness.

Your defenses highlight the strategies you use to avoid shame. The strength of your defenses indicate how painful shame can be and the extent you'll go to avoid it. Realizing the extent of your defenses helps you have compassion for how much you suffer. Realizing how much you suffer changes your perspective.

Shame isn't all bad news. The more you work with it, the more familiar it becomes. The more familiar it is, the more comfortable you become. Becoming comfortable allows you to work with shame, explore it, and experience it in different ways. Every time you work with shame, you increase your awareness of it, allowing you to act sooner. You can act before a situation gets out of hand.

Underneath shame is usually a positive personal characteristic that you embody. In fact, it's this positive characteristic that is so true it's painful to realize. Not knowing the truth all this time (for example, "I am lovable" or "I am worthy") has been painful. This realization creates a more accurate, whole you. Experiencing yourself as whole, acceptable, understood and lovable is where the emotional healing comes from.

Guilt vs. Shame

Here's how Shame Hack defines the difference between guilt and shame: Guilt is when you feel bad about something you did or did not do; shame is when you feel bad about who you are. For example: It's Mother's Day, and you forgot to call. When you feel bad for not calling, you feel guilt. Not calling is a behavior. Not calling is something you did. You feel shame when you feel bad for not calling and now you're a bad daughter. You identify with being a bad daughter. It's who you are.

Sometimes Shame Hides

Sometimes shame hides underneath other feelings. You might not feel it right away. You may have to go through a couple of feelings to get to the bottom of what you feel, as Stacey did.

My client Stacey's experience illustrates perfectly how shame can hide behind other feelings. Stacey is in her early 40's. She is a child of divorce who never took to her stepmom. They've never been close.

A couple of months before her visit with me, Stacey had gone on a weekend trip with her boyfriend Jack and his 16-year-old son, Blake. The trip was an opportunity for everyone to come together and bond as a potential family. Stacey wanted to show Blake what a cool stepmom she'd make.

At the end of a long day touring the city together, Stacey was ready to turn in. When they stepped off the subway, Blake started talking about hitting his favorite theme restaurant and then going shopping. Unbeknownst to Stacey, Jack had promised Blake dinner and shopping after sightseeing. Jack had excluded Stacey from his plan.

Stacey was tired and upset. She seized the opportunity to duck out.

"Why don't you two go on without me? I'm really tired."

"Come on Stacey, go with us." Jack turned his back to Blake and faced Stacey so Blake wouldn't see the don't-make-me-go-by-myself look. This look pissed Stacey off. She could see Jack was worn out and didn't really want to go. Jack wanted Stacey to play the bad guy and foil Blake's plan.

"No, I'm going to head back to the hotel. This is perfect. You two go get some father-son time."

"Come with us. It'll be fun."

"No guys, I'm done. Go without me. Have fun."

Stacey shared how this situation upset her. All three of them were on vacation together, trying to make some memories. She was trying to connect with Blake. Jack's exclusive, secret plan angered her. She felt like she wasn't part of the family.

Here's how our conversation went:

"Stacey, what are you feeling?"

"I'm pissed. Jack didn't tell me about his plan with his son. I felt invisible. Like I'm not a part of their family. I don't want my relationship with Blake to be like the one I had with my stepmother. I feel like I'd make such a cool stepmom. I was trying to be a family."

"You sound angry, but do you feel hurt?"

"Yep, I felt devalued. That's it. I feel hurt. It just hurts, you know. Why didn't he tell me about his plans with his son? I'm totally okay with it. I didn't want to go anyway. But at least make it my choice! Don't exclude me!"

"Do you make your hurt mean you don't matter?"

"No, it's not that. I know I matter. I'm hurt. I feel devalued. I feel less important than his son."

"Did you just say you feel less than? I thought I heard you say you feel less important than his son. Do you feel shame?"

"What? I don't know. I feel hurt."

"Feeling shame is painful and can feel like hurt. When I heard you say you feel less than. I suspect you might feel shame. Try it on and see."

She sat quietly for a few moments and felt the feelings. "Yes, I feel shame."

Stacey and I finished the Four Simple Questions. She discovered her truth: *I am loved.* This hole in Stacey's heart traced all the way back to her parents' divorce. Being left out of Jack's family plan triggered the shame and pain of feeling unloved. Stacey's story shows how a recent situation can tie to a past situation. It illustrates how finding the truth (I am loved) from a recent situation helps resolve the pain from a past situation.

Stacey's feeling evolved. (Your feelings may also evolve as you get clearer on what you feel deep down. Allow them to do that.) She started out feeling pissed off, only to realize she felt hurt. She realized she made being excluded from the family plan mean she was less important than Blake. Deep down she felt shame.

What distinguishes shame from hurt is that inner critic saying: *You're not enough. You are a failure. You're the only one.* These phrases indicate you feel shame. When you hear any of them, do a self-check and see if you feel shame.

The Lonely Kind of Shame

It's Friday, late morning. I'm driving north to visit my mom for her birthday. The drive from San Diego to Orange County takes about an hour and forty-five minutes one way. I've made this drive a lot in the last couple of years. It gives me time to think. There's something about driving in silence that lets me mull things around.

Today is no exception. I turn the radio off and merge onto the 5 North ("Interstate 5" for the Non-California readers). I'm in the mood for sulking. It's what I do best.

Over the last couple of days, I've been trying to figure out what I've been feeling. It's been bothering me, like a sunburn. It's with me, and I can feel it. I don't like it. It's uncomfortable. I want it to stop.

Yesterday morning I realized I was feeling fear. I had to get real with my fear. I had to write down what I was scared of, so I could own it. I've been feeling some fear with regard to writing this book. I was surprised to discover that my biggest fear is that after I put my book out, I will feel even more alone than I do right now. People won't get it, and I'll be the only one in the insane asylum, with no one to talk to. *A padded room for one, please. Does this straightjacket come in another color besides white? I look better in cool winter kind of colors.* I already feel like I'm at the tip of the spear. Now the tip of the spear will grow a needle nose, and I will have to walk the plank. (I know I'm mixing my metaphors, but try to go with the lonely scared feeling on this one.)

I'm feeling fear. But I'm not satisfied with that answer. This feeling is more than fear. I feel scared but also emotionally vulnerable. Like I could cry. I'm feeling and driving. *Hmm. What is this I'm feeling?*

What's scaring me and getting me emotional is feeling like I'm the only one. If I feel like I'm the only one, then what I'm really feeling is shame. *Let me try that on. Yep, shame fits.* It's just not the classic fit I'm used to, though.

Normally, shame feels like I'm not somehow enough. I'm stupid. I'm a loser. And I do feel some of that. But this time, shame feels more like I'm the only one. It's a lonely kind of shame. Not the garden variety I-think-so-little-of-myself shame.

What is this shame all about? I feel shame. Question 1 is done. What do I make that mean? I make it mean that I'm the only one. I jump to: The final set up statement of Question 3 - What do I need to know? Time to sit in the fire. Burn, baby, burn. I want to cry but I can't. I'm on the verge. But it's not happening. It's like I'm ready to sneeze, but I can't. I'm holding my breath in the "Ah" waiting for the "Choo." I'm in Ah-Choo purgatory. Come on Choo! Let me pass. Uh, frustration.

All right, fine. I'll wait. Feel some more, Dolan.

What is this shame all about? What do you need to know?

You feel alone. You feel alone.

What is this loneliness all about? Why do you feel alone?

Hmm.

Do you need to know you're not alone?

Nope, nothing, swing and a miss. Try again.

Okay, so this has to do with how your work is received, right?

Uh-huh.

So you're scared that if your work isn't received well, you'll feel even more alone?

Right.

So why are you writing this book in the first place?

This question stabs my heart. There's something to it. Like *who do I think I am?*

Go ahead, be totally narcissistic, deluded, and selfish. Just tell me the truth.

Okay. I'm doing it for the money.

Ha! Come on, you're not that deluded. This book is not going to make you famous and wealthy. Be serious.

Earlier that morning, I had listened to a TED Talks podcast by Jill Bolte Taylor, a neuroanatomist who shared her story about suffering a stroke. Amazingly, she was grateful for the stroke experience because it gave her insight into the brain, giving her insight that would've taken her years to gain in a lab. Having lived through the experience of "rebooting" her brain, she had insight from the inside as to how the brain worked.

I felt that I had worked through a lot of shame and feelings. I had figured out how to resolve shame and other feelings. I had helped other people resolve their shame and other feelings. I felt that I had insight into shame and other feelings. I felt I had the insight to share. Not because I was pompous, or an egomaniac. It was because I had worked at it long and hard and had helped other people with their difficult feelings.

Could that be it? I have insight? I'm not exactly sure what insight means. I better check. *Okay Google, define insight*. Insight (noun): the capacity to gain an accurate and deep intuitive understanding of a person or thing.

Yep, that's me. Is that what I need to know? I am insightful? My heart pings. My eyes water up. My heart weeps. That's it. That's what I need to know. I am insightful. This is why I feel lonely. Having insight is not common. Not everyone has it. That's why I've been feeling alone. That's why I've felt like I'm the only one. Oh, clarity, how I love you so!

Dolan, what's the truth? I am insightful. Yep, uhmm, that's right. I settle into my emotional satisfaction like a bean bag chair and get cozy for the rest of the drive. Time for music. I turn on the radio. Commercials. Damn it! Here we go again.

Here is LM's story.

LM: "I am capable"

When I first started seeing Dr. Mayeda, he walked me through the Shame Hack process to help me deal with years of in-law issues and leftover emotional scarring. Despite long ago forgiving my husband's parents, whenever anything came up about them or we spent time with them, those pesky, ugly feelings resurfaced.

As Dr. Mayeda assisted me through the five feelings (Sad, Hurt, Anger, Fear, and Shame), I couldn't identify which emotion I felt because years of stuffing my feelings away had left me clueless when it came time to put a label to them. So Dr. Mayeda skipped ahead to "finding my truth." He read words aloud as I sat with eyes closed, letting each one sink in. When he reached, "I am loved," emotion bubbled up inside and I was instantly crying. That was it. I needed to know I was loved.

Now, when the caller ID shows my in-laws and I get a slight tightening in my chest, I remind myself that I am loved. Knowing this means hurtful comments no longer sting as much and don't leave me wounded and feeling unloved.

I was pretty fired up after experiencing that initial breakthrough, but the task of doing the Four Simple

Questions on my own seemed overwhelming. I didn't think I could walk myself through the process without Dr. Mayeda's help. Much to my surprise, however, my defeating assumption was proven wrong. Some time later, I had the opportunity to take a writing course, but was procrastinating on enrolling. After weeks of debilitating fear, I sat in a chair in my bedroom and stumbled my way through the process, guessing again at the answers. Though I was pretty sure I felt fear, I didn't know my fear was actually shame. The question I couldn't wrap my mind around was "What am I making this mean?" so I skipped ahead and started trying on Truths one by one. I knew from experience that I would recognize the truth I needed to know about myself when I heard it. But I didn't expect that when I said aloud, "I am capable," I would instantly begin sobbing. I cried and cried, and it was profusely cleansing. I had no idea all this pain had been inside, needing to be felt. I had been living under the control of a crippling lie until I allowed myself to sink to the ugly bottom of the pit and feel what it would be like to be utterly incapable. That's when the powerful awareness took root that I was indeed capable.

This was big for me—so big, in fact, that fear continued to rear its filthy head to tell me I couldn't do something, that I would fail, that I was a failure. But all I had to do was remind myself aloud, "I am capable," and I felt empowered to move forward.

A couple months later, I found myself wanting to try yoga. I had always admired people who tried new things by themselves, but that never had been me; I was too shy. After weeks of finding every excuse not to take a yoga class, I knew I needed to figure out what I was truly feeling and what I was making it mean. In a matter of minutes, I realized I needed to know I was safe. It was so easy. Just having the understanding was all I needed. I took the yoga class all by myself, and it was incredible. And I continue to try new things on my own.

Each time I work the Four Simple Questions, I understand the process more. I make the process fit me and my needs for each circumstance. It's moldable and flexible, like the perfect pair of jeans. And each time, I feel more empowered, more complete, more confident.

One of the most wonderful, unprompted compliments I receive now is when others, including my husband, comment about the good changes they see in me. This healing and freedom should be experienced by everyone. I want everyone to know how good it feels to be free of the baggage that has weighed down their lives and held them back from experiencing the truth.

-LM

Chapter 9 – Fear

In my fifth year as a chiropractor, I traveled tc Colorado for a three-day chiropractic retreat. It was held on a vast mountain property with cabins, a cafeteria, and a large lecture hall. The property was selected for its ropes course. Think team-building exercises, a rock-climbing wall, and a telephone pole climb.

Maneuvering to stand both feet on the tip-top of a 40 foot telephone pole is pretty hairy. There's nothing to hold on to at the top of the pole except air. It's scary.

I watched as a fellow chiropractor ascended the pole. She was clearly scared of heights. She was unsteady climbing. Each reach, each handhold, each step a determined expression of her desire to get to the top. She went slowly, pausing as she climbed. Bravely, she struggled rung by rung her hands trembling, inspiring the camp with every reach upward. We circled the pole, cheering and encouraging her every move.

Her struggle was visible for all to see. Each rung was a test of her will versus her fear. Courageously, she continued till she made it to the top as cheers erupted.

Facing your fear is scary. You may have to face your fear moment by moment, rung by rung. It's okay to struggle. Every rung can be scary. But moving forward, regardless of the struggle, is sometimes what it takes to accomplish what you want. I have faith in you.

Fear Is a Natural Thing

Here's an announcement from Captain Obvious: Fear is scary. Fear is designed to keep you safe. It's nature's insurance policy for your survival.

But when it comes to feeling your feelings, fear becomes a blockade instead of a protective mechanism. Your feelings won't kill you. You are not in danger of dying from feeling them.

Feeling your feelings may scare you. You anticipate pain and shame, and especially - uncertainty. Uncertainty can be scary. I agree. But uncertainty isn't always a negative.

Hope lives on the flip side of uncertainty. When an outcome is known and predictable, there is no hope. Just like dropping a rock off your rooftop. You don't hope the rock takes to the air and flies away. No, it's going to drop like a rock. There is no hope that anything else will occur. You may fear that feeling your feelings will only bring pain and shame. But feeling pain and shame is not the final outcome. They're only the rope swing you're using to cross the divide. You got this.

You Fear Shame's Lies Are True

You might feel unlovable and secretly fear it's true. You don't want to feel this way; nobody does. No one blames you for avoiding this feeling.

When you are willing to face your fear and feel to the depths of how unlovable you are, you find that it is not true. Feeling to the depths of your feeling is like a swinging pendulum. The pendulum must swing to the end of its motion before it reverses course. When you feel to the depth of your shame, you realize it's not true; you are lovable. That moment is the turning point; the pendulum stops swinging and starts heading back.

You faced your fear of being unlovable and won. Amazing. It's a complete reversal from what you used to feel. You took your fear and turned it upside down, coming out on the other side stronger and empowered.

This life-changing shift has your name on it. All you must do is be willing to own your fear and feel.

You are capable of facing your fear, feeling your feelings, and feeling your truth. I've done it. Many of my clients have done it. You can do it too. The first time is the scariest, that's all. But with each confrontation, you get stronger, and it's less scary.

Let's turn shame on its head. There's no need to believe shame's lies. Instead, let shame be an alert that you have a truth to uncover. Shame is pointing out where you feel less-than. Nothing to fear, it's only a sign.

Facing Your Fear Is an Act of Self-love

Facing your fear and embracing hurt are acts of love. They communicate value and worth, two pillars of self-love. You choose to address your needs, and take action. You're refusing to neglect your needs. You're showing your hurting heart that you are worth the pain and suffering.

Facing fear is difficult. Respect that your fear is telling you to be careful. It's signaling: Potential pain lies ahead. But fear can be shortsighted. For example, you've broken your arm and it needs to be set. You know that setting your arm will hurt. You're already in pain. You must choose to set the bone or not set the bone. You understand the meaning of the pain setting the bone brings. Setting the bone aligns it, allowing healing. The pain from setting your arm will run its course. It's temporary. You will regain function of your arm. Soon enough it will stop hurting.

Or you can choose to not set the bone. The broken bone will stay misaligned. The bone fuses in whatever way it broke. The damage will be set in bone. Your arm may cause you pain from here on out because it wasn't set correctly. You may lose strength or function of your arm.

Not setting your broken bone comes with a cost. As does setting your broken bone. Here's the question: Is the cost of avoiding the temporary pain on the way to recovery worth it? I doubt it. Is the temporary fear and pain of feeling your feelings worth it? I know it is.

Sometimes when you face your fear you get a chance to give yourself the love you need. This is what happened for Kerry.

Scared to Lose More Weight

Kerry is a 36-year-old married mother of two. In our first meeting, she shared that she had experienced some childhood trauma. She didn't want to go into any detail. I asked her if there was sexual abuse in her background. She nodded her head yes. I'm hoping the Four Simple Questions will help her.

Kerry wants to work on a feeling she doesn't understand. Her weight and body shape have been an issue for her most of her life. She recently lost 37 lbs. She's happy about it, but doesn't want to lose any more weight.

"Kerry, you don't want to lose any more weight, which is totally okay. But you're having feelings about it. So what's up with that?"

"I don't know. I don't want to lose any more weight. I don't want to get too skinny."

"But why? What's the aversion to skinny?"

"I don't know. I don't want to get too thin. I like my curves. I like the way I look."

"What are you *feeling* about losing more weight?"

"I don't know. I guess I feel scared to lose more weight. Which doesn't even make sense. I mean what woman doesn't want to lose more weight, right? My husband says 'I don't understand.' Why would you be scared to lose more weight, right? It doesn't really make sense to me."

A Weight Loss Program That was Too Successful

"Kerry, we're talking about your feelings here. They don't have to make sense. We just want to know what you feel and what you make it mean. But maybe your feelings do make sense. Have you ever heard of the ACE study?"

"No. What's that?"

In 1980, Dr. Vincent Felitti of the Kaiser Permanente Health Maintenance Organization put together a program to help obese people lose weight through lifestyle changes. The program succeeded. The participants lost weight and felt better.

But each year for five years, nearly half of the patients in the program dropped out, even though they had been successful in losing some weight. Why were they dropping out? It didn't make sense.

Dr. Felitti checked medical records but found no common thread. He conducted exit interviews. Nothing. Then, one day during an interview, he made a mistake. Instead of asking the patient "How old were you when you had your first sexual experience?" he asked, "How much did you weigh when you had your first sexual experience?" The patient, a woman, said,

"Forty pounds," and burst into tears. Her father had raped her when she was four years old.

Dr. Felitti had never had a patient who was a victim of child sexual abuse, but he began to wonder if this was the key to the program's high dropout rate. It turns out that it was. Eventually, he and his team, with help from the Centers for Disease Control, interviewed more than 17,000 patients. What the participants all had in common is what he came to call Adverse Childhood Experiences (ACE) such as physical trauma, emotional abuse, and sexual abuse.

Survivors of ACEs try to cope with the pain as best they can. Coping often means smoking, drinking, engaging in risky behavior, engaging in indiscriminate sexual activity, using drugs, and uncontrolled overeating. Food helps people cope. It also changes a person's body. Being overweight protects the person from unwanted sexual attention. Being overweight keeps the person safe.

It Makes Sense After All

I shared this information with Kerry.

"Given adverse childhood experiences, it's understandable that losing too much weight is scary.

You're losing your protection. So feeling scared about losing weight does make sense."

"I can see that. I can relate to that."

"You feel scared about losing weight. What do you make that mean? What are you scared of?"

"I guess I'm sacred that if I lose too much weight my husband won't find me attractive."

"You make it mean you won't be attractive anymore?"

"Nah, not exactly. It's more like he'll lose interest in me."

"Like he won't pay attention to you anymore?"

"Yeah, like he won't love me anymore."

"You make it mean you're unloved? You'll feel unloved?"

"Yeah, that's it."

With Kerry's feeling and meaning established, we go over the statements for Question 3. (Question 3 is "What does that say about me?" and the statements that go with it are: I am willing to feel _______ to heal myself, I am willing to suffer to know more about myself, there is meaning in my suffering, and I am willing to endure this suffering because I needed to know I am ______.)

I handed her a list of "Truths." (Truth list available in Chapter 14)

"Please read through this, feel each word, and tell me which resonates the most."

Kerry reads through the list out loud, with a rhythm, taking her time, pausing with each word to see if it resonates.

"Lovable. Yep, that resonates. Acceptable, nope. Good, no. Worthy, no. Caring, no. Loving, a little. Powerful, no. Honest, no. Safe ..." Kerry stops dead in her tracks. She doesn't move on. Her rhythmic reading halts. She stares at the page. Her face goes blank. The room goes quiet. A few moments pass.

"Is that it? Is what you need to know, 'I am safe'?" Kerry is still taking it in. She shakes off her daze and returns her awareness to the room.

"Yeah, I got hung up on safe. I couldn't move on. It jumped out at me. Yes, it resonates."

"Is that what you need to know? Is that the truth?"

"Yes. I need to know I am safe. Yep. That's it. I just got stuck there. I couldn't move on."

"If you don't feel safe, you don't have much. It affects everything you do. I mean, how are you supposed to have any fun if you're scared all the time?"

"I know. Even when we go on family vacation, a time when it's all good, and we're supposed to have fun. It's hard for me 'cause I'm still worried that something bad is going to happen."

"I know. That's what it's like when you're scared all the time. Kerry, what's the truth?"

"I am safe."

Kerry and I go through the Healing Dialogue next. She comforts the scared and hurt part of her that's been living in fear all these years. Speaking in a kind, compassionate tone, her words get through to her heart.

I follow up with Kerry by email two weeks later. This is her reply.

Hi Dolan,

I was going to write you to update you. Man, you were right. It's like emotionally and mentally I've had a reawakening. I had that moment of "Wow life is so freaking awesome!" LOL. Like it's a whole new world that's been there the whole time but I'm seeing it for the first time. I feel like my whole internal dialogue has changed.

I've been doing the Four Questions periodically and let me tell you, I am a believer. They really do help, and I find myself being so KIND TO MYSELF as well as more patient with others. I've never been or done that in this way before.

My truth of “safe” I think has evolved even more. You're correct, it went from weight to body shape, to attractive, to loved. I don't feel that way anymore. I'm more accepting now of the weight issue. When doing the Four Questions, the word “safe” kept jumping out also as I applied it to my family and social life as well. I still have a lot of work to do though I think.

I don't think for me fear and shame are interchangeable. I feel the shame has been embedded in me for so long, and it comes up in different circumstances than fear does. I think I can also feel fear and shame at the same time.

Anyway, I'm doing okay. :)

-Kerry

Own Your Fear

When you face fears of the heart, you must be willing to have a heart-to-heart with your heart. If you're scared, own it. Downplaying or neglecting your fear actually feeds it. Owning your fear stops the feeding. You already feel scared. So just admit it.

Owning your fear helps you look it in the eye. Sometimes when you face your fear, your fear blinks first. That's all your fear has got. There's not much backing up fear except a scary presence. By facing your fear, you may realize what you were scared of is not that scary. It's like seeing a movie as an adult that scared you as a kid. For me, when I saw *Nightmare on Elm Street* as a kid, it scared me. I had nightmares for a week. I didn't want to be alone. I didn't want to be in the dark. Now as an adult, it's more like Freddy-schmeddy, meh. Can we watch *Game of Thrones* now?

Sometimes when you look fear in the eye, it will stand strong. That's fine, respect that. But do not let fear intimidate you out of what needs to be done. You can do this. Do not allow fear to be your keeper.

You may need to get a grip. Ask: Is this fear rational? Or is it emotional? Examine your fear and put it in perspective. How likely is the outcome you anticipate? Can you take action? Is there anything to do? Can you create a solution you haven't thought of before? Can you seek help or advice? Do you need to complete a task? Is this fear something completely out of your control and you simply need to make peace with it? You don't have to like it, only accept it. Accept it and learn to co-exist. Or accept it and put it behind you.

When dealing with fear about feeling your feelings, the path forward is simple. Just open your heart.

Need motivation to face your fear? Try to imagine past the hurt and fear. What is being on the other side like?

Strangely enough, it's the fear, hurt and struggle that makes your truth meaningful. You struggle. You are overcoming fear, and wrestling with your feelings is what makes your truth compelling. It makes your truth juicy.

Imagine if a classic story like *The Wizard of Oz* had no struggle. Spoiler alert: Dorothy gets caught up in a tornado and finds herself in the Land of Oz. She quickly learns that to return home to Kansas she must meet the Wizard of Oz. The Wizard is located at the end of the Yellow Brick Road. Only, in this no-struggle story, the road is a sidewalk and the Wizard is only 100 feet away. She walks over to him in under a minute and sees a man hiding behind a green curtain. She pulls the curtain back and wakes up in Kansas safe and sound in her bed. Easy-peasy. No struggle here. No fears to confront. No moments of joy. No song and dance. It's the struggle and challenge that make your truth compelling, meaningful, and worthwhile.

Feeling fear can be uncomfortable. It takes some getting used to. When you first learn to sit with fear you'll be learning to endure.

Here is Maddie's story.

Maddie: A New Perspective

On February 26, 2013, my mother admitted me to the mental hospital. I remember thinking to myself, "I can't go to school today, I can't go to school today, I can't." And I kept my promise to myself. As an eighth grader, I was at war with myself and at war with those around me. Other kids were mean. They would write about me on the bathroom stalls, stare at me, and spread rumors about me. I first got called whore when I was in the fourth grade. I still don't really know why. It started there and did not stop. And it still does not stop. What's changed is how I deal with it.

I am not a naturally unhappy person. Before my depression took over, I was lively, positive, and full of energy. But the people and events constantly erupting around me turned me from a beautiful gemstone into a dull rock, and eventually, into dust. It was December 2013, nearly a year after I was admitted into the hospital, and a week after my second suicide attempt, that I decided to make a change and went to see Dolan.

We are given a limited amount of time in our lives. We are born and then we die and that is just how it goes. I know I'm young, but I think differently than most people my age. I see things differently and I feel things deeply. I thought that I felt too much. Everything is in excess for me, which is a blessing and a curse. When it turned into a plague of feelings, I shut it off. I sat around and felt nothing (and yet somehow was still deeply sad) for almost a year until I went to see Dolan.

After two and a half hours in his office learning how to feel again, I walked out with a new perspective. But how does one catch on so fast? I think a lot of it has to do with being so tired of being tired. I was tired of writing poems that were about dying. I was tired of feeling nothing. But I was scared. Opening the floodgates for my deep feelings was dangerous. I had suffered from physical and emotional abuse from my sister, incessant bullying, and clinical depression and anxiety. I had a lot of deeply rooted emotional problems that I was refusing to deal with until I ventured into the Four Simple Questions. After a short few weeks of practicing the Four Simple Questions, everyone started to notice a difference. My mother laughed more. My father didn't sigh as often. Even my multitude of therapists noticed a change in my demeanor, a change nobody could make for me. Today, I am happier than I ever have been.

There are things you have to regard as true in your life. You must maintain integrity for yourself. And you must want to get better. Nobody else will save you. At the end of the day, when we lie awake at night, we have only ourselves. Having ourselves is the one thing that is unbreakable, and we must learn to use it. My ordeal is not over. Life is not over. There will be conflicts and there will be problems. But, when something comes up, now I know how to deal with it.

–Maddie

Chapter 10 – Learning to Endure

I come from a legacy of Japanese gardeners. Both my grandfathers worked as gardeners at some point in their lives. As a result, my dad had high-quality garden tools. Many he inherited; some he bought. I never gave much thought to having good yard work tools. I just grew up with them.

A year ago, a recently divorced friend of mine needed some help with her yard. I arrived to find an overgrown, neglected yard. No big deal, just more work than I had anticipated but not a problem. I asked her where her gardening tools were. She walked me back to the shed. All I saw was a shovel and a pickax. No wonder her yard was overgrown. She didn't have the right tools to do the work.

Whether it's an overgrown yard or feeling your feelings, you need the right tools. Learning to endure lays out the process of overcoming one of the first unpleasant feelings you run into: fear. When you first start to feel your feelings, you need to learn to endure. Inner dialogue is the tool you use to help you work past the fear.

Quivering Hamstrings

It's a rainy Wednesday evening in San Diego. A friend wants me to go to yoga with her. Her regular class is on Tuesdays, but she can go tonight because her work meeting was canceled. She likes this yoga teacher. The Tuesday night class is for beginners, so she figures Wednesday should be more of the same. I should be good. I've been cooped up all day. A stretch will do me good. *Okay, I'm in.*

I like yoga. But I'm a novice. I've only been to a handful of classes. The last class I went to was a year ago.

We got to class a little before 7:00 p.m. and spread out our mats. Since this was my first time in this class, I took a space toward the back. I always get a little apprehensive in new situations like this. Everyone is doing his or her pre-yoga thing. Some people are in full lotus position quietly sitting. Some women are limbering up like Slinkys. This should've been my first clue.

The instructor begins class. We all stand up. He names a pose in Sanskrit. The class moves into the pose in synchronicity. *Oh shit, I don't speak Sanskrit.* (The only pose I know in Sanskrit is *savasana*. This is the pose at the end of class where you lie on your back as still as can be as the teacher turns down the lights and plays relaxing music. I think *savasana* translates to *I hope I don't start snoring*.)

I'm instantly a step behind, but I follow the woman in front of me. The instructor says something else in Sanskrit. The class effortlessly moves into a plank position. I sneak a glimpse at the clock. 7:06 p.m. The class is scheduled for an hour and a half. *Damn, this is going to be a long class. I just gotta get through this.* Another word in Sanskrit and the coordinated yoga drill team moves into a new position.

Talk downward doggy to me buddy, come on! The class moves into downward dog. *Yes, something familiar.* Since I have no idea what I'm doing, I keep looking up towards the front of the room to see the instructor. It's monkey see, monkey do for me. I'm always a step behind. I realize this is *not* a beginner's class. The class is mostly women, and they look like a contortionist troupe that escaped from a Russian circus.

I'm in the back, and we're all bent over. I'm looking up to see what comes next. My hamstrings are quivering. Then I start getting eyeballed by the lady in front of me. I'm trying to make it obvious that I have no idea what I'm doing. She's not buying it. This is a medium to an advanced class. I should know what I'm doing, but I don't.

I look around, seeing more butts which gets me more eyeballs. The women in front think I'm just creeping on their butts. Suddenly, I feel like I'm Neo from The Matrix bending over backward dodging a hundred little daggers flying at me. The clock reads 7:22 p.m. *Man, I got another hour of this. Come on, savasana.*

I've bitten off more than I can chew with this class. *Man, I am stiff. I need to be more flexible.* Maybe this is a metaphor for life or something. I just carry on, falling behind one pose at a time until the class is over. I make it, quivering hamstrings and all.

The lesson: Sometimes you've just got to make it through, even if you're uncomfortable.

###

When you start to feel your feelings, you may feel uncomfortable, but it's just something you must initially get through. Learning to endure your uncomfortable feelings is an act of self-love. You are enduring unpleasant feelings to understand them and ultimately to feel understood. You are spending some time with them so you can get to know them. Learning to endure gives you practice at comforting yourself with inner dialogue. Inner dialogue is a game changer. Inner dialogue helps you cope and comfort yourself. Inner dialogue helps give your heart what it needs.

Turning Fear into Self-love

Feeling your feelings is crucial to the Four Simple Questions. Sometimes, before you start the Four Simple Questions, you may have to first deal with the fear of feeling. You have to learn to endure the first feeling, which is fear.

Alison is a 33-year-old licensed professional who attended one of my Four Simple Questions Classes. Alison met with me a week later for one of the follow-up interviews I was doing for Shame Hack. From what I gathered, Alison had a solid grasp on the Four Simple Questions. I asked her if she used the questions to discover a truth. She did.

"Great, you found a truth. Tell me about it."

As Alison told me about her experience, I grew confused. *Hmm. Her truth doesn't sound cathartic at all. It sounds flat.* Alison shared her truth in a matter of fact way. Her sharing wasn't matter of fact, as in she had completely incorporated her truth into her being a while ago. Her sharing lacked emotional energy. It dawned on me that Alison had answered the Four Simple Questions in a cerebral way. She answered each question from her head instead of her heart. That was why her truth lacked emotional impact.

"Alison, it sounds like you're not feeling your feelings." At first, she denied this. Then I explained that often when someone feels their truth, there's an emotional release. People are usually pleased or relieved in some way. But this didn't seem to be her case. Then she admitted that she didn't feel her truth.

"Okay, let's work with what you've got. We'll go over what you answered for the Four Simple Questions. What are you feeling?"

"Scared."

Alison was scared to feel her feelings. Her response to her fear was to back off and protect herself from feeling. That was why her answers were cerebral and her truth emotionally flat. She tried to think her feelings. First, Alison needed to overcome her fear before she could really answer the Four Simple Questions. I walked her through the learning-to-endure tool of inner dialogue. We speak to her heart with a compassionate, empathic and warm tone.

"Place your hand on your heart. You're going to talk to the scared part of you. Repeat what I say to your heart, okay?"

"Say to your heart: 'I know you're scared. It's okay. I'm right here. No one is going to hurt you. You are safe. I know it's scary. You can do this. It's okay. Nothing is going to happen to you. You are not alone. I'm not going to leave you. I'm right here. You can do this.' "

"Feel your heart. Are you still scared?"

"No. I'm uncomfortable. I want to run away," she said.

"Tell your heart this: 'I know it hurts. It's okay. I'm right here. I'm never going to leave you. Just let it go. You're uncomfortable. I know. I'll feel as uncomfortable as you need me to so you don't have to feel this way anymore. You are worth it. You're doing great. That's it. I'm right here, and I'm going to keep loving you.' "

I could see that Alison's discomfort had passed. Her shoulders, once tense, were now relaxed.

"How are you feeling?"

Loving the Inner Brat

"My inner brat is starting to act up. She wants to throw a tantrum," Alison says.

"Talk to your inner brat. Tell her: 'That's okay. You can be as big of a brat as you want. I'm not leaving. You are important to me. I'm not going anywhere. I'm not going to abandon you. I love you.' "

As Alison's inner brat gets the attention she wants, she begins to quiet down.

"How are you doing?"

"I feel more confident."

"Great, now say this to your brat: 'That's right! You're doing it. You can do this. You can handle this. You're fine. I'm going to keep loving you until you feel that I care.' "

"How are you feeling?"

"My fear is gone, and I'm feeling more comfortable. I feel good."

Alison had never given herself this kind of loving attention before. It made her feel more confident and comfortable with her feelings. She got out of her head and spoke directly to her heart.

In the end, Alison's vulnerability paid off. She felt good after feeling her feelings. She faced down her fear. Alison's confidence grew as a result. Alison experienced self-love, a palpable kind of self-love for being there for her heart.

Alison's case demonstrates her process of overcoming fear. Let's take a closer look at her process.

She went through several stages: fear, discomfort, urge to run, defiance, confidence, and recognition. You may go through similar stages as you confront any fear of feeling your feelings.

As Alison felt her fear, she became uncomfortable. She used inner dialogue to comfort herself. She acknowledged feeling scared and spoke to her heart, *"I know you're scared. It's okay. I'm right here."* She stayed with the fear and talked herself through it.

She felt the discomfort that fear brings and wanted to run away. But she didn't shut her feelings down, or distract herself. She stayed with her heart. She endured what her heart feels. *"I know it hurts. I know it's scary. It's okay. I'm right here. I'm never going to leave you. Just let it go. You're uncomfortable."* The discomfort transitioned into defiance; her inner brat rose up.

Alison's heart had had enough and didn't want to feel anymore. But this inner rising didn't sway Alison. She stayed right there with her heart and gave her brat permission to throw as big a tantrum as it wanted. Alison encouraged her heart and was unfazed. Alison saw the big picture her heart was unable to see. She was feeling for a purpose.

The brat's threat of a tantrum subsided; it had gotten the attention it wanted. Her inner brat wanted to protest, and her protest was heard loud and clear. Her inner brat was fully acknowledged and the protest ended. Alison's fear and discomfort had run their course.

Alison's experience illustrates the resistance you may encounter when first feeling your feelings. Learning to endure, the process of getting more comfortable feeling your feelings, is often the initial stage you go through as you get used to feeling your feelings. As Alison stuck with her feelings, she felt them rise and change. Her initial fear evolved into self-confidence.

Alison was pleasantly surprised by her outcome. It wasn't what she expected. This put her in the position to begin working with the Four Simple Questions on an emotional level instead of a cerebral level. The emotional change is what Alison wanted.

Chapter 11 – The Safe Tree

Back when I was a kid, we had a big tree in the middle of our front lawn. The other kids and I played tag on the luxurious, well-groomed grass. We ran around the yard barefoot, beads of sweat dripping from our hair. The tree was the safe zone. When you touched the tree, you were safe. You couldn't get tagged.

As we have seen, when you work with your feelings, they can feel threatening. You need a retreat, a place where you can take a pause in the action, a place to go to avoid being completely overwhelmed. You need a safe tree.

Your safe tree is an intellectual buffer. It acts as a shield when feelings become too overwhelming or intense. It provides the intellectual reassurance you need before you become willing to deal with strong feelings.

"I tried the Four Simple Questions out. But they're not for me," Sally told me.

She had attended a Four Simple Questions Class, and now we were meeting so I could get her feedback about her experience in the class.

"Can I ask why?"

"When I tried it, my feelings got too intense and painful," she said. "I think the questions are useful. But I'll use them for less intense stuff, like emotional hiccups, or something. Not for deep shame. I just feel too much."

"What do you mean you feel too much?"

"I'm really sensitive. I feel like I'm feeling all the time. It can be overwhelming. Four years ago, I got really depressed. It was bad. It affected my health. It took me a long time to recover. I don't want to go there again. That's why I only want to use the Four Simple Questions for minor things. Not gut wrenching deep things."

Sometimes, when people tell me they are sensitive and feel all the time, I find out they've been hurt. And to avoid the pain, they live in their heads, away from the hurt of their broken hearts. What Sally didn't realize was that the problem wasn't being sensitive. The problem was the lack of a better way to cope with her hurt.

"I certainly don't want you to relapse," I said. "I can relate to being sensitive because I'm sensitive too. I used to hate it. I would get my feelings hurt all the time. Being sensitive felt like a curse. But after I learned to cope with my feelings better, I changed my tune."

"Now I feel like being sensitive is a blessing. I see it as an asset. It's my gift. I'm like a highly sensitive instrument."

"This is your gift, Sally. I understand that you're apprehensive about using the Four Simple Questions. I have the utmost respect for your process. Are you willing to go through the questions again with me? This time, we'll take a different approach."

"I'm open to trying."

"You can stop this conversation at any time. You just say the word, and we'll end it. You're the boss. If it's getting to be too much, we can make an adjustment or stop. You're in control here."

"Before we even approach the Four Simple Questions, let's go over a few things. This time when you're feeling your feelings, it's going to be different than it's been in the past. You're feeling for a reason. You aren't just feeling your feelings because you're an emotional masochist and want to be in pain. There's a reason. You're willing to feel them because you want them to stop. Ready to make them stop?"

"Yes, of course."

"You're not exposing yourself to intense feelings just for the hell of it. There is meaning in your suffering."

"Sally, I want you to know you can always shut your feelings down. You've done it in the past. You still have that ability. So, if things start getting out of control you can just shut your feelings down right?"

"I certainly know how to shut them down."

I could hear the apprehension in Sally's voice start to fade. She was slowly opening up to a new possibility.

"Now, I want you to know that you can feel as little or as much as you want. If you only want to dip your toe into shame, you can. Or you can go in up to your knees. It's up to you. You can go in and out of feeling your feelings as you want. It's your choice. How are you feeling?"

"Better. Less anxious."

As Sally's anxiety faded, she began to listen.

"Sally, I want you to know that you are not alone in feeling shame. Everyone feels shame. It's just that nobody talks about it. People just don't go around openly confessing what they feel shame about. That's why it's called shame."

"That's true."

"This time when you feel shame, you won't be alone. You won't feel like you are suffering all by yourself. This time, you'll talk to yourself in a way that resonates with your heart. You can feel like someone cares. It's different now. This time, you'll benefit from a lifetime of your own experiences and wisdom. You've made it through tough times before, right?"

"Right." I could hear Sally's voice picking up. Her confidence began to rally.

"Sally, you also need to know you are safe. No one is going to hurt you. You're just not going to let that happen."

"Okay, almost done. Your feelings aren't going to kill you. You may feel like you want to die, but you won't. I know, 'Damn it!' Right?"

She laughed.

"You also need to know that you're perfectly capable of feeling understood. Even though you may have never felt understood before in your life. Got it?"

"Got it."

"So now, at least at an intellectual level, you understand things are different. You're feeling for a reason. You're safe. You're not alone. You're in control and can feel as much or as little as you want. When your feelings get too intense, you can go to this intellectual buffer zone. This is your safe tree."

"Thank you."

Feel and Retreat

Sally was now willing to reattempt the Four Simple Questions. She worked through her situation and intense shame came up. But this time, Sally navigated through her shame successfully. Instead of getting swallowed up in shame as she had in the past, she felt some shame, then retreated. Then felt some more and retreated. She moved back and forth between shame and her safe tree. Sally did this until she was confident enough to feel the shame and let it pass.

As Sally played peekaboo with shame, she kept talking to her hurt heart. She was comforting and reassuring her heart that it's not alone. This time, Sally's heart got what it needed, unlike her previous experiences. Getting your heart's needs met makes all the difference in the world when dealing with shame.

Through the Four Simple Questions, Sally discovered her truth: *I am lovable*. The shame and pain of not knowing she was lovable plagued virtually every relationship she held dear. Finding her truth, *I am lovable,* was deeply healing for Sally and affected almost every aspect and relationship in her life.

A few weeks after our session, Sally was kind enough to write the following testimonial:

Before I learned about the Four Simple Questions, I didn't know how to identify or work through the painful feelings I had carried around for more than a decade. I tried to ignore them, forget them, and numb myself out. Unfortunately, this only led to more hurt, and my body began slowly breaking down due to these toxic stuffed emotions. I became physically sicker, but was still scared to "process" or "feel." Dolan gently encouraged me to move forward, and I not only learned how to work through negative emotion, but I also learned how to understand my vulnerability in a new way—as a whole, healing person. Before, I feared facing the intense pain directly. But after the Shame Hack work with Dolan, my understanding of myself through the use of painful emotion has shifted in a life-altering way. Dolan's method includes the critical healing piece I always felt was missing.

-Sally

The Elements of Your Safe "Tree"

The safe tree is a protective mechanism that helps shield you from intense feelings. It's easy to get lost or wrapped up in your feelings. You can lose perspective. The safe tree helps keep you grounded. The components of the safe tree are:

- Admit How You Feel
- Know Feelings Ebb and Flow
- Know It's Different Now
- Know You Are Feeling for a Reason
- Know You Are Safe
- Know You Are Not Alone
- Know You Are in Control
- Be Lenient

Admit How You Feel

Before you ever start to feel your feelings, you will likely feel scared. If you feel scared, anxious, or apprehensive, just admit it. By admitting it, you're acknowledging how you feel and open to having an honest conversation. You just need to own any feelings you have about feeling your feelings. By owning them, they can be addressed and honored before you move forward. You just need to speak to your heart about what you are feeling.

I know you feel scared right now. I feel it too. It's okay. We're going to be okay.

Know Feelings Ebb and Flow

Feelings don't last forever. I'm sure you've felt happy at least once in your life even if you don't feel happy now. Feelings change. When you're in the midst of feeling your feelings, and it's really starting to suck, know that this feeling will run its course.

I know you're hurting right now. I know. This is just a feeling. I know it hurts. It will pass. Feelings always do. You won't feel like this forever. It's going to stop soon enough. I'm here with you. This is temporary, honey.

Know It's Different Now

Perhaps in the past, you were left to suffer your painful feelings alone. This is no longer the case. Now, you can have an inner dialogue with your hurting heart. Your heart will hear the words it needs to hear - the words your heart needed to hear in the past, but didn't.

You have a lifetime of experiences and wisdom at your disposal. For example, maybe feeling your feelings is starting to grind on you. You need some inspiration.

Think of something that inspires: a quote, lyrics, a dream, a story, or perhaps a movie.

Or maybe your confidence wanes. Think back to a time when you met a challenge, a personal success story. You have an entire lifetime as a resource to pull from. You know yourself better than anyone. You know what you need to hear.

Know You Are Feeling for a Reason

You're feeling this way to make a change. You are not making yourself suffer for no reason. Speak to that when you're feeling hurt.

Honey, I know it hurts. I know you want to quit. You can if you want. But I want you to know that we're feeling this way for a reason. We are feeling this way so we can make it stop. We are feeling this way so we don't have to feel this way anymore. I'm right here with you. You are not alone.

Know You Are Safe

Let your heart know it's safe. No one is going to hurt you.

You're safe, love. No one is going to hurt you. I'm not going to let that happen. You are too precious to me. You're safe. You're safe to feel exactly how you feel. It's okay. I'm with you.

Know You Are Not Alone

Sometimes feeling your feelings can be an isolating experience. This is especially true if you feel shame.

Feeling emotional pain can be lonely. Keep yourself company as the feeling runs its course. Make your presence felt.

I feel ya, honey. I know. I know it hurts. I'm right here. I'm right here with you. I'm never going to leave you. I'm staying right here. I'll never abandon you. I'm not going anywhere. You are not alone. Feel what you need to feel. There's no shame in it. These are just feelings. Go ahead and feel them. I'm right here.

Know You Are in Control

No one likes to be forced to do something painful they don't want to do. Your heart is no different. Know that you are in control of your experience. You can go as long or as short as you want. You can feel intensely or just scratch the surface. Always give your heart the choice. Just giving your heart a choice is often all that's needed to continue. Your heart wants the reassurance that it can quit if it wants. Make that okay. But deep down, your heart wants to get better or you wouldn't be doing this in the first place. Your heart just likes to know that it's participating of its own free will and not being forced. When your heart feels it's free to leave, it's all the more willing to move forward.

If this gets to be too much, we can just stop. You just let me know, and we'll stop any time. How you feel is important to me. We can revisit this later. We can take a break or move forward. You are worth it. You are so brave to do this. I just want you to know that. I'm so proud of you. This isn't easy, and you're doing it.

Be Lenient

This is a learning experience. You are learning how to feel. You are learning how to speak to your heart. You're making it up as you go. You're learning what works and what doesn't. Allow yourself this grace. There is absolutely no reason to come down on yourself. Let yourself grow.

Be extra lenient, if warmth, kindness, compassion, understanding and empathy were not your experience as a child.

Your safe tree is composed of all these components. Knowing them gives you some wiggle room when feeling your feelings.

You can feel your feelings, then pop out from feeling, by thinking about why you're doing this.

You can feel, then talk to your heart. Reassure your heart "you're not alone."

You can feel, and tell yourself how proud you are.

You can feel, and then let yourself know it's okay to take a break.

You can switch back and forth from feeling to the safe tree in whatever way works for you.

At the end of the day, you are doing whatever it takes to get you to a place where you can feel your feelings and find your truth. This is all part of the process of knowing and understanding who you are, and liberating yourself from shame.

Here is A's story.

A: It's What's Under the Anger

I haven't been sleeping. For months, I have been waking up in the middle of the night. Wide awake. Uncomfortable, ill at ease. This morning, it's 3:30 a.m. I try my mindfulness app, the guided sleep meditation. I realize I am not listening to it, I can't focus. I sit up on my meditation cushion and set my meditation timer. I listen to the bell, set an intention to focus on my breath, take a deep breath……nope.

I'm not meditating. I'm ruminating. Again. About my breakup. Still. It's been 8 months now. I am resolved with this breakup, I don't want him back, and I am truly relieved to be out of that relationship. I have even dated someone else since then. That relationship ended also, but I don't obsess about him. Why am I doing this? Why am I torturing myself with this? Why can't I get this guy out of my head? Go away! Leave me alone!

But no, I start thinking about the last text exchange. On Valentine's Day. My mother had died 3 days before. It was not unexpected; she was in a nursing home and had been very ill. I had mixed feelings. I felt sadness, regret, and guilt, and I felt empty. I'd had a rocky relationship with my mother as an adult and never fully made peace with her before she developed dementia. I knew I felt grief, but it felt distant; I felt numb and was frustrated that I couldn't feel my feelings. My boyfriend had been busy with work for months. He was always really busy and stressed with work. I was looking forward to seeing him, wanting to talk through my feelings about my mom, and getting a long hug from him. Maybe that would help me cry or help me drop into my feelings in my body.

I was out in my back yard, pulling weeds, which is surprisingly a soothing activity for me. He texted me and said he had to change our dinner plans. I told him I didn't really want to go out, I just wanted to see him. We made a plan and I rearranged my day. I went to yoga to try to ground myself. I have often found myself crying on the yoga mat; it's a great release. I sweated a lot, but no tears. When I got out I had another text from him changing plans again, but since I was in yoga class, and needed to shower, we wouldn't have more than an hour together. I texted him back that I was frustrated that he was changing plans, leaving no time for us. We went back and forth, he was fighting with his kids and we never got together. After a few more texts and emails, he broke up with me. He had been feeling overwhelmed with his work, responsibilities at home, conflicts with his kids and not having time for us, but bottom line, he dumped me. I was stunned and broken-hearted.

It took many days to register that he dumped me. I was angry, furious, but I felt numb. I sent him a text that he broke my heart. We talked on the phone, I was calm but clear in talking about the problems in our relationship over the last year and a half. I expressed my hurt and my anger that he didn't even try to solve the problems with me. That he just bailed. I had decided in advance I wasn't going to rage at him. Doing my Zen thing, non-violent communication and all that. I listened to his apology and, although I knew he wasn't being completely honest, I let it go. I know my feelings were still blocked. It felt like an empty hole in my chest. I meditated on it. The hole became a knot of pain surrounded by a block of ice. Frozen grief. Grief for my mom, grief for my lost love. I meditated on the block of ice in my chest. I held my hands on my chest and breathed into it. Day after day. It wouldn't budge. Wouldn't melt. I went to hot yoga. Maybe a tear or two on the mat, but not the thaw and the flood that I needed. I journaled. A lot. I raged on for pages and pages, purging my anger and hurt. I went back to therapy. It helped to process everything, but no thaw, no flood. I felt like I was dragging this heavy block of ice around with me everywhere. Then I met Dolan. He started talking to me about his book. We went through the Four Simple Questions on the phone. I was very intrigued. He asked me to read his draft. At this point I am in the middle of reading the book.

So here I am, lying awake, ruminating about my breakup. I am re-hashing our last conversation, when I went to his house to get all my stuff. In reality, it was very anti-climactic. He wanted to keep in touch, to not say goodbye. I said ok and just left. But I want a do-over. In my do-over I say no, this is goodbye, I never want to talk to you again, you were an asshole to me, you turned your back on me when I really needed support, after all your talk about empathy, you had no empathy for me or my feelings, you couldn't show up for me at all, you are a coward for not breaking up with me in person, for not telling me the truth to my face, for blaming it on work and your kids rather than telling the truth, whatever the hell it is ... (and I have lists of imaginary reasons in my journal, I ruminate on that all the time, everything from he never loved me at all, he doesn't want a future with me, he is afraid of another woman screwing him over, he doesn't like my kids, he feels trapped, he's in love with someone else, it goes on and on).

So after I vent my rage on him, I imagine feeling vindicated. He hears me. He's sorry. He feels bad for hurting me. I imagine feeling avenged and validated. But I am tired of this scene in my head. It leaves me frustrated. I don't feel validated, I feel invalidated. I sit up in bed and pull out my iPad. Reading is my last resort to calm myself down, distract, and hopefully go back to sleep. I am reading this book, I'm in Chapter 11, reading about multiple and evolving feelings.

I stop in my tracks. Wait a minute. Maybe my anger won't budge because it is covering up another feeling. Maybe it's covering up shame. I start the Four Questions. It's dark and quiet and I have been ruminating, so it's easy to feel my anger. It's right there. But what else? I feel frustrated. Sad. Hurt. And yes, I feel a pang of shame. I sit with it for a moment. I don't like it, I realize I have been avoiding feeling this. So, Question 2, what am I making it mean? I go through the list. Nothing really resonates. It's sort of like unworthy, but not quite. I go through the list again. What my shame means to me is that my feelings aren't important, they don't matter. It means that I don't matter. Yeah, that is it. I don't matter. I feel like I am dropping into my feelings. That's it. I don't matter.

On to Question 3. I am willing to feel shame to heal myself. I am willing to suffer to know more about myself. I need to know that I am … I look at the Truth list. I read through it slowly. I say, "I matter." That feels right. But then, I get to "Precious." That hurts. That makes me want to cry. I don't want it to be that because it really hurts. But it is. Question 4. What is the truth? I am precious. Now I can cry.

And just like that, my anger goes away. The block of ice starts melting. I feel sadness and grief. But, mostly, I feel relief. The next day, I notice I don't feel mad anymore. I want to test it, so I run my breakup scenario in my head again. Nothing. Not getting fired up. It's like, who cares? I'm bored with this story, I have other things to do.

-A

Part 2: All About Hacking

This section is about the Four Simple Questions - the step-by-step process that will help you find the meaning in your suffering. Your feelings, like shame, are causing your suffering. When you find the meaning of your suffering, it shifts – and often stops.

The Four Simple Questions

1. What am I feeling?
2. What did I make that mean?
3. What does that say about me?
4. What's the truth?

Flowcharts and worksheet available at www.shamehack.com/flowcharts.

Chapter 12 – Question 1: What Am I Feeling?

A suburban sidewalk is a perfect place for six-year-old me to learn to ride a bike. On both sides of the sidewalk is grass: front lawns on one side, the green parkway on the other. I'm off the street and when I fall, I fall on grass. My dad grabs my bike seat and runs alongside me. He steadies me. Gets me going then gives me a push. Off I go. We do this several times until I start to get the hang of it.

# # #

Identifying your feelings is like learning to ride a bike. It's something you learn by doing.

This chapter is about the first of the Four Simple Questions: What am I feeling? At the end of the chapter, you'll have an opportunity to practice the question. Until then, just read. Having the background information will help later on.

Identification

What am I feeling? It's a straightforward question: Identify what you feel. Identifying your feelings can bring you some relief if you feel anxious or overwhelmed. When you identify how you feel, you create some certainty. You bring some order to the swirling cloud of emotion. Identification acts as a calming force.

To begin, choose a conducive environment. I like to be alone in a quiet place, if possible. But I've also identified my feelings while walking around at a street fair and during a quiet drive alone. You can try different places, times and environments to see where your feelings most reliably arise.

As you begin to work with the Four Simple Questions, use a relatively fresh, current, or recent situation that's bothering you. The details will be clearer than those that happened three years ago or in your childhood. Once you're familiar with the Four Simple Questions process, you can return to those older situations.

When a recent situation triggers a feeling and you want to Shame Hack it, find one of your quiet spots and settle in. Then mentally insert yourself back into that situation and feel. Relive the situation again in your mind and heart. Make it vivid in your mind. Notice what happens in your body. Feel your feelings.

Go through each SHAFS feeling one by one. Ask yourself: Am I feeling sad? Then pause and feel. Does sad resonate? What is your body telling you? Does sad feel right? If yes, you answered question one. If no, then go to the next basic feeling, while remaining in the situation. Ask: Am I feeling hurt? Then pause and feel. Does hurt resonate? Is that what you're feeling? Make your way through all the building block feelings until you identify exactly what you are feeling.

Be honest with yourself. There's no shame in your feelings. Allow yourself to feel whatever you feel.

Don't try to figure out how you feel with your mind. Stay vigilant for the entries on "What 'Feel Your Feelings' is *Not*" (Chapter 3 – Feel Your Feelings). Ignore whatever you think you *should* be feeling. Make sure to feel it in your heart or body.

Try the feeling on like you are trying on clothes. Does it fit? Does it feel right?

If you're having difficulty identifying your feeling, it may help to use a feeling breath (See Chapter 4 – Nuts & Bolts). Remember, a feeling breath is the part of the breath after you exhale and before you inhale when there's a lull. Try feeling in that quiet moment.

Identification doesn't have to take a long time. Sometimes you know right away. Other times, it may take a few minutes, and sometimes you have to work at it. Sometimes identifying your feeling can take days. Once, it took me days to figure out I felt heartbroken. Neither sad nor hurt resonated for me. Three days after I started a Shame Hack on this particular issue, I realized I felt heartbroken - a combination of sad and hurt.

Multiple Feelings

Sometimes when you reinsert yourself into a situation, you'll find that you have multiple feelings. You might feel sad, hurt, and anger. When you feel multiple feelings, pick the feeling you feel the strongest. In the above example, if you feel hurt the most, then go with that.

There is one exception to the "go with your strongest feeling first" rule of thumb. Whenever you feel shame, go with that. Always run shame first. Shame has a tendency to be the most painful and run the deepest. So take care of shame first.

Feelings Evolve

Sometimes feelings change and evolve. This happens when there is something deep down you don't wish to feel. Often, it is (you guessed it!) shame. Shame is buried deep, and you don't want to feel it. You may be sure you feel anger, only to realize after you're done huffing and puffing, that you actually feel hurt. But what is driving the hurt is shame. Be open to allowing your feelings to evolve. When your feelings evolve and change, restart the Four Simple Questions with the latest feeling. In other words, if your feeling evolves or changes, take it from the top, restart at question one.

However, your feelings don't always evolve. Sometimes you feel hurt, and it's as simple as that. Go with hurt. You're good. And sometimes, when you're open and honest, your feelings will change as you move deeper into what you're feeling. As your feeling evolves, you should get clearer on what you feel.

Grace – A Study of Multiple and Evolving Feelings

My client Grace is in her forties and comes from a large family with five brothers and sisters. She learned to value financial independence and resilience from her single mother, Marge. Grace detailed a recent incident with her family that was bothering her.

Marge was in her seventies and needed a new car but didn't have the money to buy one. Grace's siblings suggested that those who were most financially secure pitch in for a down payment. Grace's brother, Brandon, who was the most affluent of all the siblings, said, "I'm willing to pitch in, but Mom won't accept any money from me."

Brandon's comment got under Grace's skin. With a poker face, Grace replied, "Oh? Why is that?" Brandon said, "Since I never asked Mom for any money growing up, she refuses to accept any money from me." Grace was not in the same financial position as Brandon and her financial contribution to the down payment would be a bigger burden. Grace took Brandon's comment as a dig, an attempt at one-upmanship. This exchange stirred up feelings in Grace.

Grace and I started going through the Four Simple Questions. Grace said she felt hurt and angry, and determined that hurt is the stronger feeling, so she goes with it.

"What did you make that mean? Hurt is being devalued, so how have you been devalued?"

Grace concentrated and looked inward. "I've made my brother's comments mean that I'm not capable." Another way to say it: Grace feels *less than* capable.

Grace was surprised to realize that she felt shame. When you first realize you feel shame, it may surprise you, too. Being surprised you feel shame is common.

Shame is a painful feeling. It can feel like you got your feelings hurt. Sometimes when you dig a little deeper, you realize you feel shame, not hurt. Grace's feeling evolved from hurt to shame.

Shame resonated stronger than hurt for Grace. She started over with the Four Simple Questions. She allowed herself to feel the shame.

Next, Grace began to read aloud Question 3 and the statements that follow. She began to look for what she needed to know.

I asked her, "Do you need to know you are capable?" She mulled it over. Capable resonated, but not that strong. I ask her if she needed to know she is competent. Competent resonated less than capable. I asked her if she needed to know she is worthy. Worthy resonated the strongest.

Grace shared that she felt some anger come up. She felt justified in her anger because her "brother had no right to say what he did."

I told Grace that her anger may be justified and that it's perfectly okay to feel that way. Then I said, "We should focus on your shame, because that is where the healing is." I reminded her of one of *Shame Hack's* basic concepts: Only You Can Heal Yourself. I explained that what her brother said may or may not have crossed the line. However, *she's* the one harboring all these feelings about his comments. I pointed out that at this point her brother might not even remember the conversation. So where did that leave her? Grace turned her focus back to the Four Simple Questions.

I asked, "Do you need to know you're loved?" She says no, "loved" didn't resonate. Then she came up with her own truth: good enough. "Good enough" resonated strongly with her.

I tried one more truth. "Do you need to know you're perfect?" "Perfect" also resonated strongly with her. I asked, "Do you need to know that you're good enough or that you're perfect?" Grace tried on "good enough" and "perfect" again. "I need to know I'm good enough."

Good enough worked best for her. Grace's truth is: *I am good enough.*

Grace's story illustrates a few points. She began with multiple feelings, both hurt and angry. After sitting and feeling her feelings, she determined that hurt was the stronger of the two feelings. As Grace made her way through the Four Simple Questions, her feeling evolved as she grew clearer on what she felt: hurt evolved into shame. Then, as she continued answering the questions, she felt angry again. Anger often acts as a distraction to keep away the pain of shame. Grace refocused and returned to feeling shame and completed the Four Simple Questions. In the end, Grace created a truth that worked for her.

Exercise:

Now it's your turn. Think of a situation that's bothering you – something you can replay in your mind. Reinsert yourself into that situation and identify what you feel. What are you feeling?

Chapter 13 – Question 2: What Did I Make That Mean?

I try to drink spring or filtered water. There's a water store down the street that has really good 11-stage filtered water. I like the taste of their water. I have three 5-gallon water bottles I fill up a couple of times a month. On my last trip to the water store, parking was scarce. I had to park halfway around the block.

The water store provides big plastic push carts customers can use to transport their full water bottles back to their cars. I pushed my full water bottles back to my car and finished loading. When I looked up, I saw the cashier standing right there. I was taken aback. "I'll take that," she said. I handed the cart over to her.

This was the first time I ever saw someone from the store come out to the street. I went negative. *Does she think I want to steal the cart? Why would I do that? I come here twice a month. I don't want the cart. I want the cart here. I just told her my name when I checked out.*

After my 30-second rant, I paused. *Maybe she was just being nice*. There wasn't anyone else in the store when I checked out. *She's doing me a favor and saving me a trip. I'm a turd.*

I made the cashier at my car into something negative. I made her standing at my car mean she thought I was stealing the cart. I created my own meaning from the situation; then I created a different meaning.

You Create Meaning

When you first read Question 2, you might think: *What do you mean, what did I "make that mean"?*

Here's an example. You look in the mirror and see you have a "muffin top." (A roll of visible fat above a pair of pants.) Clearly a negative thing, right? You may look at it and think, *Ugh.* You may even think, *I'm fat, I'm ugly,* or *I'm not thin enough.*

But if you had just lost 40 pounds after months of hard work, your muffin top might have a whole different meaning. You might think, *Damn I look good! I haven't fit into these pants in years,* or *I'm just 10 pounds away from my goal!* If you are a woman who appreciates curves, you might not even see the muffin top as something separate from the rest of your perfectly appropriate, lovable body. It's also possible your muffin top carries no meaning at all. Same muffin top, three different meanings. *You* create the meaning.

Here's how it works: You unconsciously perceive a situation and react with a feeling. Instantaneously you create meaning.

Perception → Feeling → Meaning

For example, you're cooking in the kitchen and the frying pan catches fire. In a split second, you perceive the situation as dangerous. You immediately feel surprise and fear, because you know fire means danger.

Fire → Surprise and fear → Danger!

Unlike the obvious meaning of fire, in your day-to-day life the link between what you feel and what meaning you created isn't always so clear. This is why you ask, *What did I make that mean?*

Meanings of SHAFS

In Question 1, you identify what you're feeling. In Question 2, you investigate what triggered that feeling. Where is it coming from? What is the meaning behind feeling, sad, hurt, angry, fear, or shame?

Use the questions in the table below to help you find the meaning. For example, if you feel sad, ask: *What have I lost? What am I losing in this situation?* Your perceived loss may be real (a pet) or imagined (love). Because you are dealing with feelings, the connection may not always be logical.

Allow yourself to feel your answer from question one and reinsert yourself into the situation. Think back to the moment you first felt your feeling. What triggered it? What did you make that mean? For example, if you feel hurt then reinsert yourself into the situation while you feel hurt. While you feel hurt, relive the situation. What hurt you? What triggered the hurt? What did you make whatever was said, not said, done, or not done mean? How are you being devalued? What did you make it mean?

SHAFS

Feeling	Questions to Derive Meaning
Sad	What have I lost?
Hurt	How am I being devalued?
Angry	What is the injustice here? How am I being threatened? (Or: Am I resisting a deeper feeling such as hurt, sadness, or shame?)
Fear	What am I anticipating (pain, shame)?
Shame	How am I feeling "not enough"? (Refer to your Shame Bucket.)

An imagined meaning can feel just as real as a real meaning.

Amber was on her way to work. It was the morning rush hour, with heavy traffic. A black Nissan Sentra merged in front of her. Amber was annoyed with the driver and switched lanes to avoid him. A couple of minutes later, the same driver pulled right in front of her again. Amber felt angry. She thought, *Why am I angry? What did I make that mean? Where is the injustice here?* Amber examined her perception of the situation. She realized that unconsciously she had made her morning commute into a race, a competition. She felt injustice because the annoying driver was cutting in front and "cheating." This is why she felt angry.

Amber realized there is no race. There are no winners or losers on the morning commute. No finish line, no prize, no trophies to win. This was simply a freeway with a bunch of cars on it moving slowly. The annoying driver hadn't done her wrong, only changed lanes. Amber looked at the clock and saw there was plenty of time to make it to work. Her anger dissolved.

Sometimes it's not what someone *does* but what they *don't do* that you make mean something. Take Holly, for example. She's single and in her late 20's. Holly had three amazing dates with Alex. Alex is in his early 30's and gorgeous, and he has his life in good order. He has a promising career. He's making good money. He's fun and down to earth, with a great sense of humor. Things were going extremely well. Holly really liked Alex.

Over Memorial Day weekend, Alex headed to Las Vegas with a bunch of buddies. He didn't contact Holly once. Holly felt hurt. She felt devalued. Although Alex's lack of contact could have been for any number of reasons, Holly made it mean Alex had lost interest in her.

What she made it mean deceived her as it turned out that Alex and his phone got pushed into the pool. And, of course, no one remembers phone numbers, so he couldn't text her.

Exercise:

In the last chapter, you thought of a situation and answered the question: What am I feeling? Now it's time to answer Question 2: What did I make that mean?

- If you feel sad, ask *What have I lost?*
- If you feel hurt, ask *How am I being devalued?*
- If you feel anger, ask *What is the injustice here? How am I being threatened?* Or *Is there something deep I'm resisting?* Figure out the deeper feeling that anger is covering up. Anger is often a secondary feeling.
- If you feel fear, ask *What pain or shame am I anticipating?*
- If you feel shame, ask *What am I making shame mean? I'm not enough. I'm unlovable. I don't belong. Refer to your Shame Bucket.*

Chapter 14 – Question 3: What Does That Say About Me?

For Christmas one year, I bought my dad the book *John Adams*, by David McCullough. I also bought him the *John Adams* HBO miniseries based on McCullough's book. The DVDs included an interview with the author. In the interview, McCullough spoke about his aspirations as a history writer. While watching his interview, I experienced something that I had never experienced before. McCullough said:

It's hard to talk about some of these things without sounding pretentious. But I think of writing history as an art form. And I'm striving to write a book that might qualify as literature. That's the aspiration. And I don't want it just to be readable. I don't want it just to be interesting. I want it to be something that moves the reader. That moves me.

McCullough's words, *"I want it to be something that moves the reader. That moves me,"* hit me hard. Out of nowhere, I got choked up. I've never been choked up out of the blue like that. I've never had my eyes fill with tears just hearing someone speak. His words resonated. I felt them. I wanted to move people. I wanted to have an emotional experience. I wanted to affirm and be affirmed.

Sometimes words hit you like that. They resonate in a way you feel in your body. They bring tears to your eyes. They put goose bumps on your arms, a lump in your throat or shiver down your spine. This is what you're doing with Question 3. You're looking for a word that resonates. A truth you can feel in your body.

Question 3 ("What does that say about me?"), builds on Questions 1 ("What am I feeling?") and 2 ("What do I make that mean?").

Now it's time to discover what you're feeling and meaning say about you. When you answer this question, allow yourself to feel whatever you make it mean. If you make it mean you are unworthy, allow yourself to *feel* unworthy. I know it hurts and can be hard. But you're worth it. Remember, you may *feel* unworthy, but you're not. What you feel is shame. And you're about to prove that you are worthy.

Here is Question 3 in its entirety:

What does that say about me?

1. I am willing to feel _______ to heal myself.

2. I am willing to suffer to know more about myself.
3. There is meaning in my suffering.
4. I am willing to endure this suffering because I needed to know I am ______.

How to Answer the Question

Let's go over each statement line by line.

Example: You feel shame.

I am willing to feel shame to heal myself.

I am willing to feel _______ to heal myself.

Fill in the blank with your feeling - sad, hurt, anger, fear, or shame - whatever you answered from Question 1: What am I feeling? You're feeling that feeling. You can agree on this statement, yes?

I am willing to suffer to know more about myself.

You're allowing yourself to feel. You're feeling sad, hurt, anger, fear, or shame. It doesn't feel good. You're suffering. You're suffering, and you want to know more about yourself, yes?

There's meaning in my suffering.

You are willingly suffering to heal yourself. You are willingly suffering to know more about yourself. You are suffering for a reason. There is meaning in your suffering, yes?

I am willing to endure this suffering because I needed to know I am __________.

Here you are. The moment of truth has come. All the time you've been suffering has led up to this. Your suffering has been festering and now it's about to get taken care of.

You're about to take center stage. All the time and effort you've put in is about to pay off. This is it!

You've been living a lie, and suffering because of it. You need to know something about yourself. You need to know the truth. Not knowing the truth has been holding you back.

It's time to discover what you need to know about yourself. You are looking for the word that resonates with you, the word that:

- Touches a nerve
- Strikes a chord

- Makes you gasp
- Chokes you up
- Pings
- Stops you in your tracks
- Hits you
- Stings
- Hurts like the truth

You want the word you experience. When the truth resonates, you feel it. Often when a word resonates it feels like the truth hurts or is bittersweet. That's what you're going for. The words sting because you didn't know that about yourself. In a few pages, you'll find a Truth List.

Take Your Time

As you make your way word by word through the Truth List, take your time. Don't rush through. Allow yourself to feel each word. It's important to feel and not think each word. Some words will do nothing for you. Others may resonate strongly. You are looking for the word that resonates the strongest. The word that resonates the strongest is what you need to know.

Read the word. Pause and feel it. Does the word resonate? If yes, write it down. If no, move on to the next word. (If a word wallops you, you're done. That's what you need to know. That's your truth.)

From the list you made, go through the words again. Feel each one. Which word resonates the strongest? You'll feel which one does. In the event you have a tie for the strongest word, that's okay. You can have two to three words. However, I strongly suggest that you feel again and see if one isn't stronger than the other. More than one truth is okay, but your truth gets diluted. Take more than one word if you must. But try to stick with one. Your truth is more powerful that way.

How strongly your truth resonates is a function of how bad you needed to know it.

Feel It, Don't Think It

When you find your truth, make sure you are feeling it and not thinking it. Do not a pick a truth because it's what you think you need to know. Just feel it. Your heart will let you know for sure. There's no need to think about it.

Sometimes when you go through the Truth List, you hear a word and it feels good. You like the way it sounds. That's great, but it's not what you're going for here. You want the truth to twinge at least. You need to feel it at some level, otherwise it's not your truth.

Adam's Truth

Adam is 50 years old and came into my office with concerns about an emotional situation from the night before. Adam was on a date with Joan, a single mom he's been seeing for a few weeks. Last night, they took in a romantic outdoor jazz concert. At the concert, they were affectionate. They held hands. They kissed. They snuggled. After the concert, they grabbed a milkshake for dessert.

At the restaurant, Joan was upset by a phone call from her son. She was planning to take her kids on an international trip. Her son just found out that she needed the father's signature to take the kids out of the country. The call stirred up feelings for Joan. The father has been absent from their lives and tracking him down would be difficult. Joan shared the news with Adam. He empathized with her.

Joan's demeanor rapidly declined. When their milkshake arrived, some of the whipped cream began to slide off. Adam licked the rim of the glass to prevent the whipped cream from dripping on the table.

"That's tacky! It's inappropriate. You are showing bad manners!" Joan lashed out, surprising Adam. Her tone became degrading, "You have a dark side. What else are you hiding from me?"

Adam is a loving soul and an old-fashioned guy. He prides himself on being a gentleman. Adam intellectually understood that Joan wasn't upset with him. He had nothing to do with Joan's change in behavior. He still felt hurt by her accusation.

This is how our conversation went:

"Adam, I hear you tell me you feel hurt."

"I do. I know I didn't upset Joan. We're having a great time up until her son called. I'm not the reason she got mean. All I did was lick some whipped cream off the side of the glass. It's not that big of a deal. But accusing me of hiding something still hurt. I'm not hiding anything from her. So I just want to know what this hurt is all about."

"How have you been devalued? What do you make it mean?" I ask.

"If I'm honest, I'd say what hurt my feelings is I felt insignificant."

"So you made it mean you're insignificant?" Adam nods yes. "Let's find out what it says about you. It says you're willing to feel hurt to learn more about yourself?"

Adam agrees.

"It says you are willing to suffer to know more about yourself?" Adam nods.

"It says there is meaning in your suffering. You on board with that?"

"I am."

"It says that you are willing to endure this suffering because you needed to know you are ... what? - Ok, let's find out what you need to know. Ready?"

"Ready." He closes his eyes.

"Do you need to know you are significant?"

"I don't know."

"Does it hurt to know you are significant?"

"No, it doesn't hurt. It feels good. I like it."

"Ok, what I want you to do is *feel* the words. We want the word to resonate. We're looking for the one that kinda hurts. You know, like the truth hurts. Let's try it again. Do you need to know you are significant? Does that resonate?"

"A little but it's not a perfect fit."

"Do you need to know you're loved?" Adam tears up.

"Yeah, that's it. Feeling loved makes part of me want to kick and scream. And another part I just want to hug."

"That's perfect. Adam, what's the truth?"

"I am loved."

At first, Adam chose the word "significant" because it felt good. But, I needed to give him clearer instructions on what we were looking for. When he felt the word "significant" the next time, it only resonated a little. This highlights the difference between *hearing* the word and *feeling* the word. When Adam heard the word; he liked it. He wanted to feel significant. But when he took the time to feel and experience the word, "significant" only resonated a bit. What really resonated was the word "loved." His truth was: *I am loved*.

When answering Question 3, look for the word that resonates, not the one you want to hear.

Let's Get Started

Ready? Let's do this. A good way to begin the search for your truth is to choose words that are the opposite of what you "made it mean" (Question 2). For example, if you made the situation mean you are unloved, then you might start with words like loved, cared for, or important.

Your truths are not limited to the list below. These are suggestions. Add whatever words resonate with you to make your own Truth List.

Truth List

Lovable	Acceptable	Good	Worthy
Caring	Loving	Powerful	Understood
Honest	Safe	Generous	Cautious
Dutiful	True	Capable	Able
Trusting	Virtuous	Hopeful	Devoted
Beautiful	Attuned	Observant	Grateful
Thankful	Visible	Loved	Precious

Helpful Hints: Dictionaries and Thesauri

Sometimes when I'm struggling to find my truth, a word will resonate, but not that strongly. Or I have a word I think *could* be my truth, but I'm just not sure.

At times like these, I look the word up in the dictionary. Looking up a definition has clarified many truths for me. When I know the definition of a word matches what I feel, the clarity pushes my truth over the hump. Other times, looking up the definition lets me know I'm off base. The word resonates less as I read more about it. I need to find a different word. Use the dictionary to clear up any confusion on what a word means.

Sometimes I feel like I'm on the right track with a truth but I'm not hitting the bull's-eye. When this happens, I use the thesaurus. For example, I feel shame and I make the situation mean I am weak. I read through the Truth List and nothing is resonating. I think, *What is the opposite of weak?* I look up antonyms in the thesaurus. I see *mighty, powerful, stout,* and *strong*. I feel each one and see if any resonate. *Powerful* resonates the most, but still not that much. Then I look up synonyms for powerful. I find *heavy, influential, mighty,* and *potent*. I feel each one of these. I find *influential* resonates strongly. This is what I needed to know. I am influential. I am not weak; I am influential. Not knowing *I am influential* is the cause of my suffering.

Travel to the Heart

There are times when nothing on the Truth List resonates and the dictionary and thesaurus aren't coming through either. You are too far removed from your suffering. You need to feel it more. You need to travel to your heart. You need to feel what your heart feels. Allowing yourself to feel at a deep level is an act of love. To help you understand what I mean, here's a little story about Jack and Diane – Head Mountain and Heart Valley.

A man, Jack, and a woman, Diane, are friends. Jack lives way atop Head Mountain. Diane lives down in Heart Valley. Jack and Diane often talk on the phone about the weather. The weather is almost always sunny and clear for both of them. They get along great.

One day, a dense fog rolls into the valley. Diane begins to tell Jack how scared she feels driving in the fog. Jack doesn't understand her fear since he's never experienced fog way up on the mountain. Diane says that the fog is scary because she can't see.

Jack responds, "Is there something wrong with your eyes?"

Diane says, "You don't understand Jack, you need to drive down to the valley to experience what I'm talking about."

Jack loves Diane and agrees to drive down and visit. Jack encounters the thick fog and feels scared that another car will smash into him on the freeway. Jack arrives safely at Diane's home. Diane feels touched by Jack's gesture. Now, Jack understands exactly what Diane is talking about having experienced the fog. Jack relates to Diane that sometimes in the mountains, he experiences something similar to the fog, dense clouds.

Sometimes you have to travel to your heart to understand what it's feeling. Traveling to your heart will give you more clarity. Allow yourself to feel whatever you make it mean at a deeper level. This will help you better understand the nature of your suffering. A better understanding helps your truth stand out more.

Sources of Inspiration

When you get stuck, the best thing to do is remain open. Remain open for the truth to come to you. Sometimes the truth just needs to simmer before it reveals itself. You've already planted the seeds of truth in your mind. When my truth isn't coming to me despite all my efforts, I take a break from the pursuit. I move the question to the back of my mind. Then I go about my business and let the truth come to me.

Your truth may be revealed in surprising ways. It could come in a song you hear, a video clip, something you see on TV or in a movie, something you come across on-line, or a passage from a book. Your truth may find you when you're talking with a friend. So be open. Revisit the question, what you need to know, from time to time. Be patient. The truth will come if you let it. It can feel like the name of something right on the tip of your tongue. You just can't get it at the moment. Hours or days later, the answer comes to you when you stop trying so hard and let it come to you.

Sometimes you just get stuck. You can't seem to find a truth that resonates. This happens to me too. After I try my normal tricks, I look for inspiration from outside sources. Sometimes I play with angel cards. Angel cards are like tarot cards but they're all positive or inspiring thoughts. Sometimes I pull a card that hits home and my truth becomes crystal clear. I also use another set of cards called OSHO ZEN tarot that helps with mindfulness and meditation.

Sometimes, I ask the *I Ching*, also called *The Book of Changes*. The *I Ching* is one of the oldest books in the world. To use it, you write down your question. Throw three coins six times, then based on the sequence of the coins' heads or tails you look up your answer in the *I Ching*. The answers were written in ancient Chinese poetry. If you want to use the *I Ching,* I suggest a simplified version. *I Ching* answers can be complicated.

Exercises

Carrying over from the previous chapter exercise. You answered Questions 1 and 2 for a situation that is bothering you. Now answer Question 3: What does that say about me?

I am willing to feel _______ to heal myself.

I am willing to suffer to know more about myself.

There is meaning in my suffering.

I am willing to endure this suffering because I needed to know I am ______.

Chapter 15 – Question 4: What's the Truth?

Have you ever fed a dog a treat? You hold the treat in your hand. The dog comes up and devours a little bit of canine heaven. Then the dog just stares at you waiting for your hands to magically create another treat out of thin air. You have to give the dog the all-gone sign. You open your hands. Splay your fingers and turn your hands palm up, palm down like a blackjack dealer leaving the table, while you say *all gone*. The dog needs a signal to know it's done.

Your head, like the dog, needs a signal when it's done. This is where Question 4 comes in: What's the truth? It's a signal to your head that your process is complete.

Answering Question 4 is straightforward. It's another fill-in-the-blank.

Personal Truth

Let's talk about the word "truth." For our purposes, when I talk about "truth" or "your truth," I'm talking about a *personal* truth. A personal truth is something that is true for *you*. Something that is accurate for *you*. I'm not talking about a universal truth that is true for the entire universe all the time.

Here's what I mean by personal truth. Say you like spicy food. You appreciate a little kick in your dish. This is your truth. You like spicy food. Your truth is independent. It stands alone. This isn't a universal truth. This doesn't mean that everyone must like spicy food. If someone else doesn't like spicy food, does this take anything away from your truth? Of course not, that's their truth. No one is made right. No one is made wrong. It's just a different experience, with different tastes.

Say your truth is: I am lovable. This is your personal truth. It stands alone. When you know you are lovable, that's the truth for you. Someone else may intentionally or unintentionally infer that you are unlovable, but that's of no consequence, because you already know the truth. You are lovable. That's all that matters. Your truth is yours to celebrate and embrace.

Michelle Learns Her Truth

Michelle is in her late 30's. She's short in height but big in heart. She's a successful sales professional and in the middle of planning her wedding. She's looking forward to marrying her best friend and confidant, Rob.

While Michelle was discussing her wedding plans with a friend, she had a panic attack. Her heart started to race. She couldn't think. Her palms got sweaty. She was overwhelmed with the cost, duties, and expectations of the big event. Michelle felt fear. Under normal circumstances, Michelle was a calm and even-keeled person who didn't fluster easily.

Michelle was uncomfortable with the large cost of the wedding. She felt pressure and didn't want to disappoint anyone in her or Rob's family by not having a big wedding celebration.

Michelle and Rob were covering the entire cost of the wedding themselves. If it were up to Michelle, she'd have an intimate destination wedding with only immediate family and friends. But big weddings were a tradition in both their families.

Michelle worked her way through the Four Simple Questions. She discovered her truth was: *I am responsible*. This was the meaning of her fear. Spending such a large amount of money for a one-time event scared her. It felt so irresponsible.

Responsible resonated with Michelle because she was reliable and dependable. She was especially financially responsible and frugal. Michelle's upbringing had deeply ingrained the value of financial independence. The cost of the wedding went against her frugal values. Acting in opposition to her values reeked of irresponsibility and scared her.

Michelle didn't know her truth that she was, in fact, a responsible person. She and Rob could afford to spend on their wedding. They were both gainfully employed, with robust careers, and made good money. They set a budget and managed to stay within it. Knowing she was responsible helped shift her fear.

Michelle was able to move forward knowing her truth: *I am responsible*. Michelle faced her fear, answered the Four Simple Questions, and embraced her truth. Michelle's payoff was getting back to being herself and enjoying her upcoming wedding.

The truth is I am ______

Last question! You're almost there. You're ready to answer Question 4: What's the truth? The answer is a fill-in-the-blank: *I am* ______. It's simple. Recall the truth you discovered in Question 3: *I needed to know I am* _____. Carry that answer over to Question 4.

If you discover that you needed to know "I am lovable," then Question 4 goes like this:

What's the truth? I am <u>lovable</u>.

That's all there is to it. Here's another example. You discover that you needed to know "I am precious." Then Question 4 goes like this. What's the truth? I am <u>precious</u>. Here's one more. You discover you needed to know you are virtuous. Question 4 goes like this. What's the truth? I am <u>virtuous</u>. Get the idea?

This question asks: After all the work, feeling, and suffering you've put in, can you whole-heartedly accept your discovery? Is it true? What's the truth? The truth is, I am _____ (what you needed to know). Having you say the truth (I am _____) brings closure to your mind. Your heart knows the truth. Your heart felt it. Now your head can be in agreement. You just put yourself through the Four Simple Questions to come to this conclusion. When your head accepts the truth, you're done.

Question 4 may seem anticlimactic. And, well … it is, a little bit. Your struggle and the work are over. There's nothing left to do but enjoy. It's a bit like making tapioca pudding. Questions 1 through 3 are the making of the tapioca pudding. The pudding prep, the cooking, the tasting to get the flavor just right. Now you have pudding. The process of making the pudding is over. All there's left to do is enjoy.

Humming

This is the final step in the Four Simple Questions. Don't worry, it's not more work. It's fun. It's time for humming. After you discover your truth, you may need to help it get into your body. You may need a little reassurance. You help your truth get in your body by humming.

After you say your truth: I am lovable, you hum. You say, *yep, mm-hmm. That's right.* As you hum, you nod your head up down, just like you are nodding your head yes.

The whole thing looks like this:

What's the truth? I am lovable. *Yep, mm-hmm. That's right.* Nod your head yes while you are humming.

Put some soul in it. It's fun. If you want to be dramatic and act up, go for it. Here's your chance. There's just something about humming and nodding that helps your truth get in your body. It's like you are talking yourself into it. You start to believe it.

Humming is a little goofy, but it's fun to be goofy. Sometimes it's exactly what you need to take the edge off and lighten the mood. By ending with humming, you're acknowledging that dealing with feelings can be serious but that there's still room for fun. It's reassurance that working on your emotions doesn't have to be a total drag. Celebrate: you made it. You discovered your truth. Yep, mm-hmm, that's right!

True Colors Shine Through

Your truth changes you. It changes what you believe about yourself. Changing what you believe changes how you feel. You change in an organic way from the inside out. You feel different on the inside. You begin to present yourself differently on the outside. When you own your truth, your vulnerability to what you once made it mean disappears. You no longer need to guard, defend, obsess, or shame yourself to avoid this painful feeling. People's judgment carries less sway.

Why? Because you now know the truth. You know yourself, and if someone doesn't get that, it's okay. Just like when you hear a funny joke and laugh. You get it. You burst out in laughter. Someone who doesn't get the joke, doesn't laugh. That's okay. They just don't get it. Same holds true with your truth.

As you change, you may find some people less than supportive. Your old buttons that people once pushed may not work anymore. As you grow stronger in knowing who you are, the ways in which people used to shame, hurt, or manipulate you may no longer work. These people may protest or they may not. Either way, once you change, people are forced to adapt to a new you. Other people may be completely supportive of the changes you are making. They may applaud and admire your effort. Your true colors now shine through.

Here We Go Again

You've completed the Four Simple Questions. You're feeling good. Then your old feeling starts creeping back. An event or experience triggers your old feeling. While you may get triggered, your old feeling usually isn't as strong.

When you get triggered, just remind yourself of your truth. I am lovable, *yep mm-hmm that's right*. Or whatever your truth happens to be. What usually happens is reminding yourself of the truth dissipates your old feelings. Remember: You've already taken care of this. Your heart forgot the truth and is getting anxious. But once you remind your heart, it relaxes and the feeling will go away. When in doubt remind yourself of your truth. Yep, mm-hmm, that's right.

You've answered all of the Four Simple Questions. What now? Sometimes when you answer the Four Simple Questions, it's a hum dinger. You got deep. You resolved something painful and you may need some healing. The next chapter focuses on healing and gives you the words you need to help make yourself whole. It provides some of the words your heart needs to hear. Hearing healing words often helps you make peace with your suffering and move forward with grace.

Part 3: Healing Dialogue

This section is about the Healing Dialogue, which teaches you how to talk to your hurting heart in a way that makes it feel touched, loved, comforted and understood.

Chapter 16 – Talk So You Feel It

Have you seen the movie *Jerry Maguire*? It stars Tom Cruise and Cuba Gooding Jr. Cruise plays a superficial sports agent who has a change of heart.

There's a famous scene from the movie when Jerry, played by Cruise, is fired from his agency over lunch. This triggers a race between Jerry and his now-former agency to retain clients. Jerry wants to talk to as many clients as quickly as he can to get their commitments.

Jerry is racing along until he gets on the phone with Rod Tidwell, played by Gooding. Rod wants to talk to Jerry. Rod wants Jerry to *earn* his business. Jerry wants to get Rod's commitment quickly and move on.

Rod's not having it. He keeps Jerry engaged in conversation while Jerry watches his phone lines go from all lit up to hang-ups with each passing second. Rod forcefully tells Jerry what he wants. As Jerry is dying on the line, Rod keeps asking for more personal attention until all of Jerry's clients have committed to his competition. Jerry is sunk.

Rod still carries on. He signs with Jerry but wants Jerry to embrace his family motto: Show me the money.

Jerry halfhearted says, "Show you the money."

Rod wants him to say it like he means it. To say it like he feels it. Rod urges Jerry to say it louder and louder with more and more enthusiasm until Jerry's screaming, "SHOW ME THE MONEY!!! SHOW ME THE MONEY!!!"

Your heart is like Rod. Your heart needs you to talk so it feels it. It wants you to *show me the love*.

Your heart wants you to show it the love. Show you understand how it feels. Show you know how to move it. Show you know how to comfort it. Show you know how to heal it. Talk so you feel understood.

To heal, you must feel your feelings. No feel, no heal.

Show Me Don't Tell Me

Why should your heart listen to you? Your heart has been making do without you this whole time. If you want your heart to listen, you need to show it you understand how it feels. Showing your heart you understand is the key to emotional healing. Only after you demonstrate understanding will your heart relax and listen. Only after you demonstrate your understanding will you feel understood. How do you do this? It starts with feeling your feelings.

When you feel your feelings, you feel what your heart feels. You'll feel your heart's pain. Then you both know how much and how deeply it hurts. Knowing is understanding, and understanding is knowing. You show your heart you understand because you went there with it. You understand the significance and extent of the feeling.

Your heart believes you now. It knows you know. Your heart will listen to you now. Your words can get in. The words you speak come from a place of authentic compassion. That's real compassion from someone who knows and understands. Not someone giving lip service but someone who's been there.

When you talk to your heart, try to connect with it. Connection is the language your heart speaks. Your heart doesn't speak logic or rationality. Your heart speaks feelings. Speak in a way your heart feels. Touch your soul.

Have you ever been moved by someone's words? Have you ever been moved by a gift? Or by an act of kindness? Your soul was touched. Touching your soul is what you want to do when you talk to your heart. You want to embody the spirit that touches your soul. Sometimes touching your soul is saying something gentle and loving. Sometimes touching your soul is absolute honesty about your circumstances. Sometimes touching your soul is tough love. It depends on the situation.

Whether your touch is gentle, honest, or tough, what's important is that you feel moved. Feeling moved means you feel respected, valued, and loved. These feelings show your heart the love.

Self-talk

Self-talk is a means to comfort yourself. You can use self-talk any time during the Four Simple Questions. Maybe you need some comfort when you are feeling your feelings. Go ahead and comfort yourself. Talk to your heart. Maybe you need a little comfort in figuring out what you feel. You feel scared. Give yourself words of encouragement. Maybe you struggle with Question 2: What did I make that mean? Talk to your heart. Take yourself by the hand and walk through the situation step by step together. Maybe you discover your truth, and it wallops you. Take a moment and be with your heart. Let it know it's going to be okay.

Appreciate the significance of your truth. If it hurts, talk to yourself about how much. Talk to yourself about how much this truth means to you. Show you understand. Let's say your truth is *I am lovable.* You may have never felt lovable in your entire life. Feeling lovable is a huge deal for you. Feeling lovable may be something you've always wanted to feel but didn't. Now you do. Appreciate yourself for making that a reality.

If you have a harsh inner critic, self-talk can help you change your inner voice. You are in essence changing your inner critic to an inner affirmer. The way you talk to yourself changes over time with practice. It can quickly happen when you're diligent.

You can learn how to do self-talk from the Healing Dialogue sample. It shows what to say to your hurting heart. After a few times, you'll find that you adopt your own voice. You say what works for you. Say what is natural for you. Say what resonates for you. Say what you need to hear. Say what makes you feel understood. Talk so you feel it.

Healing Dialogue

The following is a sample of a Healing Dialogue. This Healing Dialogue is used after you discover your truth. In this example, the truth discovered is a big one:

I am lovable. This truth is liberating, yet painful to acknowledge.

For this example, we are going to call your ailing heart by a nickname, Ally. The dialogue is made more intimate by using an affectionate nickname. (If you don't have a nickname you like, use your name or any term of endearment that resonates with you.) Ally is feeling hurt and her truth is I am lovable.

Step 1: Let Ally know that you know how she feels.

Ally, I know you're hurting, honey. I know you feel hurt. I feel you. I know. I see you. I hear you. I know.

Step 2: Demonstrate you know how Ally feels.

Place both hands gently over your heart. If she feels sad, then feel her heavy heart. Being in the same space establishes a connection between Ally and you. Ally feels reassured. Make Ally feel you care.

I know it hurts, Ally. I know it's painful. I know, honey. I know you're hurting. (Cycle this message as necessary. If Ally has several feelings, let her know you know.)

I know you're feeling hurt and sad. I know you're lonely. I know. I know this feels overwhelming. It's hard and I'm right here with you.

Step 3: Reassure Ally that things are okay and she'll be okay.

It's okay, Ally. Everything's going to be okay. You're okay, and everything's going to be all right. I know it hurts. You're okay.

Step 4: Encourage Ally to let the hurt go.

To release and allow the hurt to run its course and exit her body.

It's okay. Just let it go. I know it hurts. It's okay just to let go. I'm right with you. You are not alone. I'm never going to abandon you. You're safe. I'm not going let anyone hurt you. It's okay. Just let it go. That's it. Just let it go.

For our purposes "let it go," means to release the hurt and not forget or ignore it.

Continue to say: *I know. I know it hurts, honey. I know it's painful.* (Do this as long as your heart needs to hear it.)

Say *I know it hurts* as much as you need. It helps your heart come to terms with its pain. As long as Ally is in the feeling, stay there with her. Give her the time, comfort, and support she needs to let the feeling pass. If she is crying, let her cry. After all, she's been holding back her tears all this time. Allow her the freedom to be herself, even if she's sad. Ally doesn't have to appease anyone at this point.

Step 5: Let Ally know you know the truth.

Honey, you are lovable. You are loved. I know the truth.

Step 6: Reassure Ally she's been misunderstood.

I know that you are lovable. I know that you are loved. And that's all that matters. I know you want other people to know that about you, and it hurts that they don't. But that's not up to us. What's important is that I know that about you. That's what matters most. That's all that matters. I know.

Step 7: Let Ally know how much you appreciate her.

I know it's been so hard for you to feel this way. You've been so brave in sharing this. I just love how you never gave up. I'm so proud of you. I know you always do your best, and that's enough. You are enough for me as you are, and you always will be. I love and appreciate you, just as you are. I love you, Ally.

You can pick and choose what steps work best for you. Edit the statements how you wish. Whatever you say, make sure you show your ailing heart you know how it feels. Say what helps demonstrate you know how your heart feels. This demonstration helps you feel understood.

The tone you take is important. Do your best to communicate a tone of warmth and empathy.

The sample Healing Dialogue is a model to build from. Adopt your own voice. Adopt your own sense of style. You may hear healing words or sayings that catch your ear from friends, co-workers, books, movies, songs, video clips, magazines, or what you see and hear out and about. Whatever you use, make sure it touches your heart.

Here are a few helpful ideas to keep in mind when you talk to your heart:

Talk to yourself and know you're not alone. Know you're not the only one who feels this way. Everyone has feelings. Just because people aren't sharing theirs with you doesn't mean they don't feel them. You are not alone in your feelings. Connect with your heart in a way so it doesn't feel alone.

Know you are part of something larger than yourself. This can be part of your family, community or organization. Or this can be part of humanity. Or being a part of something bigger can be something spiritual.

Knowing you are not alone and are a part of something larger than yourself makes for a nice container to work within.

Cry Me a River

Give yourself the freedom to just feel. In Step 4 of the Healing Dialogue, you encourage Ally to let the hurt go. When you're in that moment, go for it. Curl up in the fetal position and cry yourself a river. Play healing music. Music that speaks to your heart. Music that moves you. Music that makes you cry. You know, stuff from Adele. Then have at it.

While you cry a river, talk and comfort yourself. When your emotional window opens, take advantage of it. Sometimes when you feel your feelings, you get scared. A feeling catches you off guard and bites you. You react and slam your emotional window closed. After you steady yourself, that window may be hard to reopen. Getting back to the feeling you were just in is hard sometimes.

You are right there, ready to cry, feeling emotional, ready to let the hurt come out. At that moment, try and allow it to happen. I know it hurts. I know it's hard, but talk yourself through it. You'll get better at keeping your emotional window open with practice.

Getting back to that feeling place doesn't always happen. When you're in that cry-your-river-of-tears place, go for it. Use Steps 5 to 7 in the Healing Dialogue to finish up. Your catharsis is complete.

Comfort – Checking In

When you start having feelings, sometimes all you need to comfort yourself is a check-in. You notice you're starting to have feelings. You check in with yourself. *Hey, what's going on in there? Are you okay? What are you feeling?* Then take a moment and feel.

Maybe you feel sad this morning and need a couple of minutes to cry. You cry for a bit and then you're good for the day. Maybe you're irritated, and you just have to own it, so you don't become passive aggressive. Maybe you feel scared, and you just need to check in before your imagination and worst-case scenario loop starts playing continuously. Just check in and talk yourself down from the ledge.

Sometimes when you start to have feelings all you have to do to comfort yourself is remind yourself of your truth. Let's say you start feeling anxious about an upcoming meeting. You've already discovered the truth about this meeting. You discovered: I am lovable. Remind yourself: I am lovable. *Okay, I know you're feeling scared. But the truth is I am lovable, yep mmm hmm, that's right. Okay? Okay. Good.*

Perhaps you check in and feel a big feeling brewing. If it's not a good time to address your feeling, let yourself know you plan to take care of it later. *I know that just sparked some shame in you. I can feel it. We're at work right now. So now's not a good time. We'll take care of it when we get home. Okay?* Just checking in and acknowledging your feeling can give you the comfort you need in the moment. You can work through the feeling later.

This was Becky's case. She had to put her feelings on hold till a better time and place was available.

That Girl

It was spring. The perfect time for a southern outdoor wedding. Becky, in her late 30's, traveled with her husband to her brother, Tim's wedding. Tim's wedding was picturesque. All the guests were impeccably dressed. The altar stood on perfectly groomed grass overlooking a lake. The scene was cut from a bridal magazine. Becky took it in. She saw the long line of bridesmaids standing up for the bride. Then a sense of deep sadness overcame her.

This was the wedding Becky imagined for herself as a little girl. The scene was beautiful. But what struck her heart was the seven bridesmaids. The bridesmaids were all childhood friends of the bride. They grew up together. They knew each other their whole lives. These lifelong friendships were what Becky always thought she'd have, but they never happened.

Becky grew up as a military child. The family's frequent moves gave her little opportunity to establish long-lasting friendships. This loss came to light when she saw the parade of bridesmaids. Coupled with the sadness of not having lifelong friends was the hurt she endured being the new girl.

Becky was the new girl more often than she could count. Moving from community to community is tough for anyone, let alone a little girl. Being the new girl wasn't easy. Becky had run in to her share of cliques. She was left out and excluded from established friendship circles. The long line of bridesmaids triggered her sense of not belonging.

Becky's sadness began to soak in deeper. But she didn't want this. She was at her beloved brother's wedding. Her entire family was there. She wanted to avoid a meltdown. She was already feeling emotional seeing her brother make his vows. She didn't want to be *that girl* at the wedding.

In the quiet moments of the ceremony, Becky started talking to her hurt heart.

Honey, I know you're feeling so sad right now. I can feel it. I hear ya loud and clear. I know it hurts, honey. This was supposed to be your *wedding. This is the wedding you wanted.*

I know. You're feeling disappointed. I know.

But honey, this isn't the time or place to get into it. We can get into it later. We can hash it out back at the room. Okay?

I know it hurts, Bec. And we'll get to it. I promise. But we don't want to ruin Tim's wedding do we?

No.

Ok. Let's try and enjoy ourselves for now. Look at Tim. He's so happy. We're so proud of him. Let's be here for him, ok?

Becky's heart got a much needed hug. Her heart got the attention it wanted and was content for the time being. Her heart felt acknowledged and was willing to wait to work through her feelings. Becky went on to enjoy the celebration with Tim, her new sister-in-law, and the rest of her family.

When Becky returned to her hotel room, she shared how she felt sad during the nuptials with her husband. She talked about moving around a lot and how she didn't have childhood friends. Becky's intimate conversation drew her husband in. Becky's husband demonstrated loving kindness and patience. After they talked she felt loved and cared for. Becky got her needs met at an appropriate time, place, and manner.

Other Things You Can Do

Say What You Need to Say

Sometimes you just have to get things off your chest. You need to say your piece. You need to speak your truth. You have to tell it like it is.

Other times, you need to own up to your own wrongdoing. Your error in judgment. To take responsibility for your contribution to a breakup, or divorce, or something that went sour. And sometimes, you never got a chance to say what you needed to.

When there's something you need to say, writing a letter is a great option. For me, when I write a letter it's for *my purposes*. I'm writing the letter to say what I need to say with complete honesty. I have no intention of sending the letter. This gives me the freedom to say whatever I want. I may rant, rage, shame, scold, insult, beg, grovel, plead, ask, tell, admit, honor, or expose. If I am writing a letter to send, I might not write my real feelings down. I might feel more inhibited.

Nature's Antidepressant

Exercise is nature's antidepressant. Nothing beats exercise for getting your happy neurotransmitters going. You don't have to start training for a half marathon or anything – unless you want to! Just get out and do some walking. Go get your blood moving a little.

Sometimes when you're down and feeling vulnerable, the last thing you want to do is go outside. That's okay. Take some time to recover. Be patient. Be gentle. Give yourself a recovery period and then take a 15 to 30 minute walk and enjoy some fresh air.

There are numerous studies that support the benefits of exercise on mental health. Take advantage of what exercise has to offer. Get nature's antidepressant working for you.

Help from a Pro

Working with a mental health professional has many benefits. A therapist can be a good sounding board for you. They can give you insight into your feelings. They can help you feel understood. A therapist can help you answer the Four Simple Questions, all while holding a safe space.

You must seek immediate help if you have destructive, violent, harmful, or recurring thoughts or feelings towards yourself or others. Get help if your feelings or lack of feelings (feeling numb) are getting to be too much for you. Talk to a professional. That's what they're there for. Everyone can use some help now and then. You're not alone. I had help, lots of it. There's no shame in getting help.

The Issues Are In the Tissues

I'm not talking about KLEENEX here. "The issues are in the tissues" is a phrase my chiropractic kinesiology mentor says to me. He means that sometimes emotions get stuck in the body. By helping the body function better, the emotional issue sometimes gets resolved. I'm an advocate for chiropractic and chiropractic kinesiology. Getting your body healthy can help you feel better emotionally too. It's easier to feel better emotionally when you feel better physically. Your mind and body are connected.

Showing yourself authentic compassion not only helps you emotionally, but it may also benefit your body as well. The research findings of a 2014 study, "*Self-compassion as a predictor of interleukin-6 response to acute psychosocial stress,*" appeared in the journal *Brain, Behavior and Immunity*. The research set out to find out if self-compassion is associated with lower levels of stress-induced inflammation. Their "findings suggest that self-compassion may serve as a protective factor against stress-induced inflammation and inflammation-related disease." The authors, Julia G. Breines, et al., also stated, "elevated levels of inflammation can increase the risk of a range of diseases, including cardiovascular disease, cancer, and Alzheimer's disease."

Answering the Four Simple Questions and performing a Healing Dialogue may offer more than just feeling better emotionally. It may help you stave off inflammatory-related diseases through the practice of authentic self-compassion.

Signs of Getting Emotionally Healthy

The following are some signs of getting emotionally healthy. Some of these signs may already apply to you. Others you may aspire to reach. If a sign appeals to you, circle it. You now have something to work toward.

- Remove shame from your core
- Appreciate all your feelings (the good, the bad, and the ugly)
- Give yourself authentic compassion and patience
- Accept yourself
- Comfort yourself with self-talk, give yourself tender, gentle loving
- Become more playful, more light-hearted. Creativity comes easier. Remaining present becomes easier.
- Become more aware of your feelings. More able to talk about your feelings and not take them out on other people. More able to act them out (if need be) in a safe and productive (non-harmful) manner. Able to channel your anger in an appropriate manner.
- Become more able to express compassion for other people's feelings without necessarily

being affected by them. You don't have to fix, attend, or rescue someone from his or her feelings.

- Replace grandiosity with genuine confidence
- Accept, appreciate your body. Ideas of healthy, beautiful, strong, and sexy come from you.
- Replace belittling yourself with nurturing yourself
- Replace shame with pride
- Replace feeling like an outcast with a sense of belonging
- Replace loneliness with connection
- Become comfortable with feelings; stop resisting them

My Broken Heart Discoveries

This section contains two complementary stories. The first story details how I stumbled upon what happens when your heart breaks completely. The second story is about how I learned my truth: I adore.

Story #1: Broken Heart to New Heart

What becomes of the brokenhearted
Who had love that's now departed?
I know I've got to find
Some kind of peace of mind
Maybe

What Becomes of the Brokenhearted, Recorded by Jimmy Ruffin,
Written by William Weatherspoon, Paul Riser, and James Dean

Writing letters is a tool that helps me put my feelings into words. A letter forces me to sit down and put my thoughts and feelings on paper.

Several years ago, I wrote a letter to an ex-girlfriend so I could feel complete with her. In other words, energetically close the connection in my heart and be done. The purpose of this letter was to own my part in the outcome of the relationship.

I had tucked away the pain, shame, and embarrassment of my past behavior in that relationship. While that relationship was decades old, I still burned a flame for her. I knew the relationship was ancient history. That there was no way we would ever be together again. Nor would she or I want to be. We're on different paths. We were young then. Now we're different people.

I hadn't thought of her, even in passing, for decades. So why did the flame still burn? I wrote my letter, painstakingly owning all my behavior. Exchanging my victim card for the responsibilities of ownership. I could feel my heart break. I remembered this pain. I never wanted to feel that pain again. I used a protective strategy for my broken heart. *Don't touch it! It's fragile.* I didn't want it to break anymore. Any disturbance or agitation to my broken heart was too painful. It was as if my heart had a tear exposing all the raw nerve endings. *Stand back; you're getting too close.*

Of course, my broken heart didn't work. It didn't love like it was supposed to. It was broken.

As I typed the letter, I felt my tears fall on the coffee table. It was painful to admit how I wronged her. It was painful to admit how much I loved her. It was painful to admit how much I needed her. It was humbling to admit how my insecurities ruined something beautiful. Sadly, I ruined it on purpose. Relationship sabotage strikes again. I never wanted to admit these things. But now I was, and my heart was breaking completely.

While writing this letter, I started to feel even worse. My flame moved from the unconscious to the conscious realm. I didn't feel bad for burning a flame for her. But I saw how burning a flame for her made my heart unavailable to other women I dated. It was unfair to them. The guilt, gravity, and shame settled in. I descended to a new level of low. Shame oozed out of me.

Here's what I pictured: I was sitting at a romantic restaurant. A perfect table set for two. I sat in one chair and the place setting across from me had a tent card reading, *Reserved*. The seat was reserved for my ex. I didn't even realize I was doing this. Waiting for something that was never going to happen. In the meantime, and it's shameful to admit, other women could join me at the table, but they couldn't sit down.

That seat was taken. It's reserved. They have to stand there. That seat and my heart belonged to another.

I've protected myself by reserving that seat and not allowing any other woman to sit. I thought I'd prevented my heart from breaking any further. But, as I wrote this letter, my heart completely broke. Then over the next few months, something unexpected happened.

A new heart grew in place of my old broken heart. I had a new heart. I could feel a heart that could love again. I never imagined this would happen - that the way to deal with a broken heart was to let it break all the way so a new one could grow to take its place. When you let your heart break completely, you give yourself a chance to love again. Can letting your heart break all the way be painful? Of course, but why protect a broken heart that can't love? Why protect the pain and deny yourself the love?

This new heart grew in harder than the original. Version Two was more experienced, cautious but not cynical. I thought a harder heart was a better heart because it wouldn't break as easily.

Wrong.

I learned after Version Two broke that a soft heart is harder to break. A soft heart is flexible and yielding. A soft heart can absorb a blow and survive while a hard heart will break. A soft heart will help you avoid a broken heart.

When you answer the Four Simple Questions, you will run up against your broken heart at some point. This is where much of your pain comes from. Many, many things can break your heart. But don't let a broken heart prevent you from enjoying the love that's in your heart. The love you have to give. The love you have to share. You are worth letting your heart break completely if need be.

Story #2: I adore

For the last two weeks, I've been on a *feel the love kick*.

Two weeks ago, my buddy Kevin and I had a conversation about the Universal Laws or the Law of Attraction. Normally, he sets an intention for the day as part of his daily practice but says that lately life has been too chaotic to get the practice in. I've heard of the Universal Laws before; my source was the movie *The Secret*. I'm on the fence about the laws. I wanted to hear what Kevin had to say.

Kevin shared his belief in the importance of setting an intention. "If you don't set an intention, the Universe will fill that intention for you," he said. Kevin owns a small printing business.

"I set the intention that my customers will pay on time, my employees will work together in harmony, and that the shop will grow effortlessly."

"Tell me more about the intention part. How do you do that?"

"When you set an intention, you have to set it like you believe it. As if it has already happened. This lets the Universe assist with your intention. Your intention lets the Universe know what you want so that the Universe can manifest it. You're only bound by what you believe."

I entertain the thought of practicing the Universal Laws. I'll give it a shot. *Sure, why not*? I'm setting the intention to feel more love. Let's see what happens.

Every morning for the past two weeks, I have said a little intention prayer. I ask that my heart be filled with love. And that my heart comes from a loving place when I write. At night, before I go to sleep, I say another little gratitude prayer for the love I felt that day.

To my surprise, it's working. For the last two weeks, I'm feeling the love more and more. Now, I try to be conscious that other people want to feel love and have love to give. I start seeing people differently. I see them as beings of love. Now I'm curious about the love they have to give. Now when I approach people, I find myself more drawn to them. I'm feeling the love.

In the middle of this experiment, I get my third patient referral from Taylor. Taylor and I have been casually dating for the past couple of months. We haven't made any commitments. We see each other once a week or maybe on the weekend. She's a single mother, and her schedule needs to be flexible because of her daughter.

Despite my experiment, I feel that Taylor has been less available over the last few weeks. Days when we normally get together, we haven't. We're not texting like we used to. Our normal pattern of communication and dating has changed. It feels like she's drifting away.

This is probably not the right time to talk with Taylor, but I don't care. I'm feeling the love. I'm all wrapped up in my kick. I want Taylor to feel the love too. I want her to know how much I appreciate her. I want her to know I think she's beautiful. I want her to know how much I appreciate her referrals. To know how much her support and referrals mean to me.

I've never been with a woman who believes in me as strongly as Taylor does. She believes I can help people. She's out there talking me up. She's championing me. I'm touched. I want to show her the love. I set my intention.

Taylor and I have enjoyed our time together. We've had our laughs. I'm attracted to her. I like her. This feeling the love thing has got me all revved up. I'm swirling in love. Without saying it directly, I'm going to declare my love for her.

I call her, and we briefly chitchat. We cover the how-was-your-day stuff. I shift into my love gear.

"Hey, I just really wanted to thank you for the referrals. Your friend, Gary, called me today and he's coming in next week."

"Oh, you're welcome."

"Your referrals mean a lot. I've never had someone I'm dating advocate for me like that. I'm touched you believe in me. I'm touched you're out there talking me up. I appreciate it. No one I've dated has believed in me like you do. I just want you to know how much I appreciate it."

"Ah, thanks. I believe in you, Dolan. I think you can help people. I met Gary on Tinder. We went out last Sunday."

TINDER...*Errrrrr,* I hear the sound of screeching tires in my head. My momentum just slammed on the brakes. Ouch, arrow in the heart. *Keep beating, heart!* Cold sweat. Electricity pulses in my veins. I wasn't ready for that. *Just keep breathing.*

"We were at dinner and Gary told me he hadn't been feeling well lately. He's in a messy divorce and has a lot of emotions about it. I kept thinking: *Dolan could help you with that.* Your name came up like three times."

My mouth is as dry as a judge handing out a life sentence. *Say something, Dolan. You need to say something here.* I want to hang up the phone and break out the first-aid kit on my heart. *Speak.*

"Oh. I didn't know you were on Tinder."

Shit. Why did you just go there? You didn't want to go there. The words just jumped out of my mouth. *Fuck, this is going to be a train wreck.*

"I'm not taking myself out of the dating pool. We've made it clear that we're just casually dating."

My heart breaks a little more.

Oh, no, no, no. I'm tap dancing, trying to recover. *Be mature about this, Dolan. Come on.*

"You're right. We haven't made any commitments."

"I'm busy. I hardly have any time to myself."

Ouch. I can't believe this is getting worse. But it is. Taylor has time for "randoms" on Tinder, but not for me.

"Between, my job, my daughter, and taking care of the house, I don't have any time to myself. I need my alone time, Dolan."

Exhale, whew. *Just breathe. Maintain, Dolan.*

"Oh no, it's cool." The pitch of my voice is high, like when you tell someone after you tasted their bland cooking that 'it's good.'

"I understand. I get it."

"I like what we have. Seeing each other once a week and maybe a weekend here and there. I'm good with that."

The last remaining herd of wild bison just stampeded my heart and ego. But, damn it, I set the intention to show Taylor the love and I'm going to do it. This couldn't come at a worse time. Brace yourself. I'm going down in a blaze of glory. Someone hand me a match. *Fuck it. I'm going to blindside her. She's already on the way out. This will be good practice.*

"So Taylor. I gotta tell you that I called with the intention to gush on you. I've been consciously trying to feel the love for the last couple weeks. And I was so touched by you believing in me. I'm just full of love for you. I feel lucky that we're dating. I know we are dating casually. But I just have to admit that hearing you're on Tinder hurt a little. And it's okay. I'm totally cool with it. I understand. These are my feelings, not yours. They're my responsibility. I just wasn't expecting it. And I'm glad you told me."

"You know we're not serious. I don't want a boyfriend right now."

"I know. I just wanted to gush on you. I'm not asking you for anything. I'm scared I might sound clingy and needy, right now. But I'm not trying to be. I'm just gushing. I'm enjoying what we have, and I was so touched by you believing in me. I wanted you to feel the love. I wanted you to know I appreciate you."

"That's sweet."

I'm professing (unsolicited) my love for Taylor. I take her comment as condescending. Should I sit, lie down, and roll over too so she can pet me on the head? *Dolan, stop. Come on. Feel the love. Focus.*

"I just wanted you to know I've got a lot of love for you. And, you mean a lot to me. That's all."

Right now, I'd be more comfortable stepping into a 100 percent wool jumpsuit with a full outbreak of chicken pox. Dead air fills the line. *Did I just get lucky with a dropped phone call? Could she have missed what I just said? Can I still save face?*

"Hello?"

"Still here."

Crap. I'm not going to say anymore. Cringe worthy silence rings out.

"Well, I'm glad we had this talk. Thank you for sharing."

"I'll tell you what. I'll leave the ball in your court. If you want to continue dating just text me. Sound good?"

"Sounds good."

"Good night, Taylor."

"Good night, Dolan."

I get off the phone. I'm having second thoughts about going down in flames. You don't have to graduate from Stanford to know that wasn't the smartest play.

My feelings are hurt. I tell myself: *Dolan, this is good for you. I know you're hurting. That's okay. Just go with. It's okay. It's good for you. You can handle it. It's not that bad. It's good practice.* I take a few deep breaths to let the whole hot mess sink in.

I need something to do. I have a writing project I need to work on. I'll do that. I sit down at the computer. I start writing. My mind begins to wander.

Did I do something wrong here?

No, I don't think so. I mean, it was awkward and all. But I didn't do anything wrong. I didn't hurt Taylor's feelings or anything. I got my feelings hurt. But that's about it.

I focus on writing again. I get a paragraph down.

So why did you do it then? You didn't have to. You could have easily said nothing. But you just couldn't help yourself. You had to declare your love. And you did it despite your hurt feelings. So why did you do it? You know you just ran her off, right?

I've been on the receiving end of someone declaring their love. When the feelings aren't mutual, it's uncomfortable and awkward. *You knew this, and you still did it. Why?* I feel like I'm wrestling with some shame. But that's not exactly it. Something is stirring, but I don't know what.

I guess I just wanted Taylor to feel the love. What's wrong with that?

Nothing.

You even pulled a kamikaze just to show her. Dolan, you just wanted to show her love. Dolan, you're just full of love.

I stun myself. I can't believe that I said *I'm full of love*. It takes my breath away. My heart pings. I freeze. I want to cry.

Realizing that I'm full of love unintentionally touches on some of my deepest shame. Feeling full of love is the exact opposite of feeling shamed to the core. I wasn't expecting that. *I'm full of love*. It's hard for me to believe. But I'm feeling it. It's resonating.

I wonder if there's a truth in this somewhere. What is it? *All I wanted was for Taylor to feel the love. I wanted to adore her. And I did. Is that it? I adore?* I look up the definition.

Adore: to love or admire (someone) very much; to regard with loving admiration and devotion

The dictionary definition didn't resonate. I had my own definition in mind. Here's my definition.

Adore: to love freely regardless of fear

My definition resonates. That's me. That's, unknowingly, what I've been striving to do.

I always wanted to love and adore the woman I'm in a relationship with. But I've never been able to do it. I've always been too scared. But, I did it this time. I loved on Taylor even knowing that it wasn't going to end well.

Now, I believe I can adore the woman I'm together with. My excitement level rises. My senses are heightening. Life is swirling around inside, tickling me. I'm so happy. My soul is smiling.

I'm bursting with joy. Happy as can be, like a well-fed baby after a diaper change.

I get a visual. I'm all alone on cloud nine. It's ironic because I have a thing about feeling understood. I want to feel understood. I need to feel understood. But at the moment, I'm so happy. No one is going to understand me. And I don't care. No one is going to get me. And I don't care.

I haven't gotten this high from a truth in a long time. There's no way I'm sleeping tonight. Oh well, I'll sleep tomorrow. *Enjoy your happiness, Dolan. Smile.*

Sometimes a broken heart needs to completely break before you can grow a new one in its place. It's how you go from "shamed to the core" to "I adore" and loving freely regardless of fear. I believe this is the real secret: having a heart that quickly regrows. A heart that can pop up like Whac-a-Mole. As soon as your heart gets knocked down, a new one pops up. *Whack, whack, whack.*

Your heart can't be defeated. It keeps coming back undeterred, full of love, again and again.

Exercise

Once you make it through the Four Simple Questions and know a truth, it's time to talk to your heart. Place your hand on your heart and read the Healing Dialogue script directly to your heart. Try to put some feeling in your words as you connect with your heart. Speak in a way that your heart can feel.

Go back to the signs of getting healthy and make notes. For each sign, write whether you haven't done it, are doing it, or want to do it. This will give you a baseline to see all the gains you make as you continue working with Shame Hack.

Chapter 17 – Kid Gloves

Sometimes in life, your heart gets beat up. It gets stepped on. It gets smashed. When times like this come around, you need a boost beyond the normal Healing Dialogue. You need to handle your heart with kid gloves. Your heart needs a little tender, gentle loving. Not always, but sometimes, giving your heart some extra loving care and attention is all you need to heal and feel whole again.

Guilty Pleasure

Back in the early 2000s, there was a TV-dating show called *Blind Date*. The premise of the show was simple: Two people meet for a blind date while a film crew follows them. You got to see all the awkwardness, comedy, and, sometimes, chemistry as each date unfolded. Most of the dates were cringe-worthy fiasco. That's why it was so fun to watch. I also enjoyed the one-liner word bubbles that popped up over the video footage. This was my guilty pleasure. I'm a bit embarrassed to admit it. But it's true.

I have a healing guilty pleasure that I'm also embarrassed to admit. But it's worked for me, so I'll share it with you. Sometimes, when I need a little extra healing, I'll work with an inner child doll, which in my case is a stuffed animal—a stuffed gorilla to be exact. It's embarrassing to admit that I'm a grown man playing with a stuffed animal, by myself. *There, I said it.* I can even admit that I still find my little gorilla useful from time to time.

Here's Looking at You, Doll Face

Sometimes it's nice to work with something tactile. Something you can feel. Something you can put your hands on.

A doll or stuffed animal provides a nice cuddly squishiness that you can press into your chest. It's interesting how having something to hold on to can help you feel a little less alone.

I use my squishy gorilla occasionally when I'm trying to feel something deep. When I feel alone. Or when I feel sad. My doll helps me access feelings. It keeps me company.

You can also speak to your doll as you would your hurting heart. When I first started practicing a Healing Dialogue, I would talk to my doll out loud. Speaking out loud to my doll revealed my tone of voice. I could hear my impatience and irritation.

If the Healing Dialogue isn't making it into your heart, you may want to consider working with a doll. Try speaking out loud to your doll. You may need to change your tone of voice before your heart believes your sincerity and lets your words in. Try talking to the doll as you would your own child, niece, nephew, or best friend's child. This may help you find compassion and patience. Sometimes the hardest person to give kindness to is ourselves.

While I use a stuffed animal, it's just an option. You can use your hands over your heart, a photograph, an object of affection, or something with sentimental value. It doesn't matter what it is as long as it matters to you. I just prefer something cuddly.

Tender, Gentle Loving

A healing booster I use when I'm down is tender, gentle loving. Tender, gentle loving helps when my heart is hurting and needs some extra TLC. My heart needs to be handled with kid gloves. Tender, gentle loving means spending some quality time with my hurting heart.

For me, it's easiest to give tender, gentle loving first thing in the morning upon waking. I wake up, the room is dark and quiet. I'm warm underneath the covers. My mind is quiet, and my body is relaxed and rested. I'm peaceful. I can feel and concentrate.

I grab "Little Do" (my stuffed gorilla) and place him on my chest. My gorilla is about a foot tall. He's the perfect size and weight to lie comfortably on my chest. Just enough mass so I can feel him, not too much that he labors my breathing. With him directly on my chest, he slowly starts to heat up.

I don't talk to him out loud like I once did. Now my conversations are directed to my heart where the spirit of Little Do lives. I've grown attached to my stuffed gorilla, like a favorite coffee mug or pen over the years.

He gives me something tactile to work with. There are times when you just need to touch something physical. You're so wrapped up inside of yourself. It's nice to have something to squeeze and press on your chest to ground you. Having my stuffed gorilla on my chest helps me focus my awareness where my heart is.

Here are my thoughts on how I get into tender, gentle loving.

I take deep breaths, sinking into a more perceptive mode. *Feel Dolan.* That's it. Just breathe and feel. *What's going on here? How do I give myself tender, gentle loving? Okay, how do I get into this? Hmm.*

I got it. Think newborn babies and puppy doggies. You want your heart to melt. As if the photographer, Anne Geddes, just shot the most adorable photo series of babies and puppies sleeping all over each other. Just eat that up, nom, nom, nom. This is the spirit of tender, gentle loving. Picture a newborn puppy, adorable and tiny in the palm of your hands. Think how adorable, fragile, precious, and delicate this young life is. Imagine your hands glowing with love. Now, instead of the puppy, imagine your heart. Let your heart take in that same love. Send your heart the message that you too are tender, precious, and delicate.

Focus on the feeling of being touched in a tender, gentle, loving way. The feeling is not about the actual sensation of being touched. Focus on the feeling that you get from being touched with love, warmth and attention. The security, the closeness, the caring, the intimacy. Give yourself the love you need.

Your heart goes out to you. I know that sounds funny, but that's what you're doing. Your heart goes out to you the same way it would for your best friend who is suffering. Let your heart feel for you too. Let your heart have empathy and compassion for you too. You need to feel loved too. You need tender, gentle loving too.

There's a meditative quality to giving yourself tender, gentle loving. You and your heart are together in a meditative bubble. A safe and nurturing place away from the outside world. You interact with your heart. You can speak to it. You can touch it. The meditative-like quality provides the quiet, peaceful space where you can touch your soul.

When you are given tender, gentle loving, you comfort yourself. You give the closeness of touch, a feeling of caring.

We've looked at the healing capacity of tender, gentle loving. But tender, gentle loving can also be used to create a connection with your heart. Just focus on being with yourself. Just hang out. Don't do work in your mind. Don't start making plans or problem solving. Don't have mental conversations with other people. Don't think about other people. Just be with yourself in your heart space.

Acknowledge and feel, acknowledge and feel. This is the cycle. This is the process. Talk to your heart like she's your little bestie, an endearing friend. When you feel and acknowledge, you create an authentic understanding for your heart. Tell her: *I know how you feel little buddy. I feel it too*. This helps her feel understood.

As I was working with my gorilla on how to explain tender, gentle loving, my heart twanged. I felt resistance. I was caught off guard as if someone had just dumped a box of rocks into my gears of progress. I thought: *What's up with that? What's going on here?*

Here's how my check in with my heart went:

What are you feeling? Really? You feel threatened? Okay. *Why? What's up with that?*

My heart doesn't want to reveal our secret life together. We worked hard to get here. We worked hard to figure out how to heal and comfort ourselves.

Let them figure it out on their own. Little Do doesn't want to share our secret-healing weirdness.

I feel some more. He doesn't want to share our connection. Our intimate personal moments. The intimacy behind closed doors when we're all alone. There's no one else in the room. Just our thoughts and feelings, our conversations between us. He doesn't want to reveal what we say to each other. He doesn't want to share the love. He wants to keep it for himself. I get it.

But Little Do, this is not how love works. Love is not something you keep. Love is something you give. Where would we be if no one shared his or her love? Would you want to live in a world like that?

No.

There's not a limited supply of love. We're not going to run out. I know it hurts you to give love sometimes. But you do it anyway. That's one of the things I love about you. I know you want a return on it, sometimes. But that's not giving love. That's trading love. Love is not currency. It's a gift. And yes, it's not always easy to give. You can hope to receive it, but you can't demand it. It doesn't work that way. When you demand love from someone when they don't want to give it, what they give you is not love. It's resentment. You are trying to force them against their will. Do you understand?

Yes.

By feeling your heart and talking to it, you're communicating, *I'm right here. What is it? What's wrong? Oh, I feel that too.* You are making your presence felt, like being touched while you fall asleep. Your voice and attention demonstrate your presence. You're helping yourself feel complete. You're helping yourself feel understood.

How to Give Tender, Gentle Loving

You can give yourself tender, gentle loving at any time. It's just a matter of connecting and comforting yourself whenever you need to. There are no rules. You're the boss.

Often, tender, gentle loving is used when you feel sad, alone, or vulnerable. You want your heart to feel your presence. You want your heart to feel like someone is there for it. You've experienced a loss. You feel alone. You need some tender, gentle loving.

To begin, find yourself a safe and peaceful space. You may be there for 10 to 40 minutes. You want to be comfortable so make sure you can sit or lie down.

You may want to work with an object of affection like a stuffed animal, doll, pillow, picture, piece of jewelry, and so on. The object is just there to give you something tactile to squeeze, touch, or hold. If you're at a loss for an object, you can place your hands over your heart.

Name your object of affection. Something that warms your heart. Naming the object helps give you someone to talk to and feel for.

Press your object into your chest a couple of times. You want to get out of your head and into your body.

Take a couple of deep breaths. Quiet your mind and settle in. Let go of your to-do list for now. You're going to be productive in a different way.

Breathe and feel. *What is bothering you*? Breathe and feel. *What is going on in there*? Breathe and feel. *Are you hurting*? Think precious, tender thoughts. Think puppies, kittens, or babies. Think whatever it is that melts your heart. Open your heart. Send this tender, loving energy to your heart.

Acknowledge and feel. Maybe you feel sad. Acknowledge it and feel it. You want to know how sad you are. Maybe you feel hurt. Acknowledge it and feel it. Maybe you feel alone. Again, acknowledge and feel.

Speak to your heart. If you are sad, speak to that. Speak tender, gentle, loving words of acknowledgment and acceptance. Give your heart the tender, gentle, loving compassion it needs. Your heart wants to feel better. Help it by acknowledging what it feels.

Ah, honey. I know you're sad, baby. I can feel it too. I'm right here with you. I know it hurts to love. We'll be okay. I know. Let's just feel this out together. I know. You're not alone. I'm right here. That's right. I'm right here. Ah, honey. I know. That's it. I know.

Avoid ignoring or neglecting your heart's feelings or wants. This just adds to your suffering.

When you feel your heart's suffering, you send your heart out to it. Treat it as you would a dear friend who is suffering.

Comfort your heart with your presence. Focus on yourself. Show up for yourself. This is not a time for blaming, rehashing, ruminating or focusing on what others may have done to you. No, this is your heart's time. A time to give your heart the love, attention, and affection it deserves. It's not ax-grinding time.

Give your heart your presence. Your full undivided attention if only for a couple of minutes. You can feel it when you do. It's satisfying.

As you discover your truths, you may run into some hiccups such as: what does it mean if I keep getting the same truth? Am I doing something wrong? Or what to do if many words are resonating? Or I'm having a hard time accepting my truth. What should I do? These three scenarios are discussed in the next chapter, *Further Down the Road*.

Chapter 18 – Further Down the Road

My dad was an engineer. He was a planner and thought through the different scenarios his project might encounter. He thought about potential problems and how to avoid them.

As you make your way further down the road with Shame Hack and the Four Simple Questions, you may encounter a couple of common scenarios. Here are the scenarios:

What does it mean if you keep getting the same truth over and over?

What do you do when many words resonate?

What if you are having a hard time accepting your truth?

We're going to check back with one Shame Hacker you've met before - Kerry - and introduce two new Hackers - Fredee and Heather - to see how they negotiated the challenges of each of the scenarios above using the Four Simple Questions for healing and growth.

Let's look at their stories.

Kerry Continued – One Truth, Again and Again

Sometimes you need to know the same truth under different circumstances. Kerry is the woman who felt that it wasn't safe to lose weight. Her truth, *I am safe,* kept jumping out at her. Different situations trigger the same meanings. If your truth happens to be *I am lovable* four times in a row, so be it. This doesn't mean that you did the Four Simple Questions wrong the first time. This doesn't mean that you don't know your truth. You just need to learn it in a different way. What's most important is that your truth resonates. (I've gotten repeat truths before, too.)

Kerry's fear of losing weight may have been connected with needing to feel safe due to childhood trauma. She had felt unsafe for most of her life. Her truth, *I am safe,* was something that Kerry needed to know in a couple of different ways.

We met one month after her introduction to the Four Simple Questions. She wanted to share her breakthrough on a situation that had haunted her marriage for the last five years. First, she shared more of her background.

From the time Kerry was a little girl, the mantra *men are dogs* was ingrained in her. Her father cheated on her mother. Her mom had illegitimate kids. Her grandfather had an affair. Infidelity extended to her aunts and uncles as well. There was a pervasive lack of trust in the marriages she witnessed growing up. Kerry's takeaway messages: Men are bad. You got to fight to keep your man.

Kerry began dating her husband Alan at the end of college. After graduation, Alan left their Southern college town for a job in San Diego. Kerry and Alan did the long-distance thing for months.

Kerry grew up in the South and wasn't about to move away from her family unless she got a commitment from Alan. Alan proposed. They got married.

When Kerry moved to San Diego to join Alan, she discovered he'd been cheating and lying to her. Here's how our conversation went.

"Women just started coming out of the woodwork. He had all kinds of women on the side."

"How did you find out?"

"A woman found me on Facebook. I thought: *Who is this woman? Why is she sending me messages on Facebook? Why does she know my husband?* Then I started snooping. I found all kinds of text messages and emails. He was involved with multiple women. I was so hurt. How could I trust him now? He'd been lying to me our whole relationship. I thought I'd found my dream man, a man that was different. But, he's a lying cheater just like the rest of them."

"Your husband just proved you right, that all men are dogs."

"Exactly. This happened five years ago. All the trust was gone. I've been living in fear that he's going to cheat again. He was remorseful and sorry. I forgave him, but I still felt scared. Whenever he was late, I'd wonder where he was. Is he cheating on me? Why doesn't he pick up his phone? I've been terrified with fear, just frozen."

"That was five years ago, and he's changed. He checks in. He asks permission before he goes out with the boys. We've got kids now, and he's so much better at communicating. But if he's gone too long, I panic. My mind spirals out of control, and I automatically think the worst."

"I've done that. My imagination runs away with me too. So how does this relate to the Four Simple Questions?"

"A couple of weeks ago, Alan went to the store. He was taking longer than normal. The fear started going. Is he cheating? Where is he? When he gets home, we have a huge fight. And then he breaks down crying. He says, 'I hate that I did this to you. You must feel miserable living like this. I would die without you. If you left me, I would just go home and die.' I told him don't say that."

"I know he's changed. He's given me no reason to think he's cheating. I even snoop his email from time to time and check. I log into his phone records and look up phone numbers I don't recognize. I forgave him, but I just can't shake this feeling. How long can I keep punishing him? This can't be healthy for our marriage. So I decided to do your Four Question exercise."

"So what were you feeling?"

"I was feeling fear. I was terrified."

"What did you make that mean?"

"I made it mean I'm rejected. That I'm not good enough."

"That you're not good enough?"

"That I'm not enough woman to keep my man happy. I'm scared that I'm going to get ambushed by another woman who's going to take my happiness and security away."

"So you feel shame?"

"I guess I do. It always goes back to shame. I'm scared. If my husband cheats, what does that say about me as a woman?"

"I think you feel shame and it scares you. So you feel shame, and you make it mean you're not enough as a woman. What did you need to know?"

"I am safe. 'Safe' just keeps jumping out at me. I need to know I am safe. Then I started talking to myself. I kept telling myself *I am safe. You are enough. Your husband loves you. I am good enough.*"

"Did you have an a-ha moment when you discovered you're safe?"

"Not then. But two days later, I was driving alone. Out of the blue, I said 'If he cheats, it's not the end of the world.' I couldn't believe those words came out of my mouth. I've been so terrified of him cheating. Then that just popped out of my mouth."

"Suddenly, I didn't feel so scared. I didn't feel like I was in danger. I didn't feel the threat. Now I don't feel like I have to try to control everything. If it happens again, then I'll deal with it. I'm not saying it's okay. There'll be hell to pay. But it's not the end of the world. It's not the end of our marriage. I'll deal with it. We can move on. We've always had a rocky foundation. He's done a lot to put my mind at ease. Now I feel like I've properly dealt with my part."

"That's fantastic. What a relief. Do you trust him?"

"Now I trust that I'll be ok. Even when he changed, I still didn't trust him. Even when he acted right, I didn't trust him. I wondered how I would ever get over his cheating. I worried that I might push him away to another woman. It's been a roller coaster. He goes out, I panic. He walks in, and I calm down."

"So, do you still feel threatened?"

"I was good for two weeks, and then he went out again. I felt the panic starting. The 'what if's' started going. But I just talked to myself. I told myself: *I am safe. My husband loves me. And I'm enough.* Then I brushed it off."

"I love my husband. And he loves me. He makes me want to be a better person. We respect one another. We put the other person's feelings first. That's why I think we're gonna make it."

Kerry worked with the Four Simple Questions, and discovered the same truth, 'I am safe,' twice - but from two different situations. It doesn't mean that her first truth was wrong. As long as the truth resonates, then it works. It's what you need to know. Your truth can be 'I am safe' five times in a row. This just means you need to know you're safe in five different situations.

Fredee – Many Words Resonate

Let's say your list includes *lovable, safe, valuable, precious, powerful, capable, virtuous, beautiful,* and *softhearted*. What do you do? You go back to the list and *feel* each word. Then take the words that strongly resonate and compare them with one another till you find the word that resonates the strongest. That's what Fredee did.

Warning: the following story contains a graphic sex scene.

I first met Fredee at a friend's barbecue. She had a friendly openness and ease about her. Fredee and I had an immediate, organic level of comfort with each other. I mentioned I was writing a book about liberating yourself from shame. She was intrigued and wanted to talk about a recent situation. We set a date to meet.

Fredee, 39, a survivor of childhood sexual abuse, had divorced her physically, emotionally, and verbally abusive husband two years before. She had been focusing on her children since then. Tragically, abuse was in Fredee's comfort zone; it was comfortable because it was familiar.

Fredee's father had abandoned her and her mother before she was born. Her mother was a drug addict with a live-in drug dealer boyfriend who sexually abused Fredee for eight years; her mother denied the abuse was happening all eight years.

When she grew up, Fredee was raped while serving in the military. She shared with me the humiliation of the pelvic exam to collect evidence for the rape kit and the further humiliation of the intrusive questions she had to answer prior to the court martial proceedings. The jury ruled against her. She left the military as soon as she could with an honorable discharge.

Despite all the trauma, Fredee was now thriving. Her eldest daughter was in college, and her other two children were flourishing in high school. Fredee had a successful career and owned her home. She had spent two years putting her life back together piece by piece.

She was dating again and wanted to talk about what happened the last time she had sex. This is how our conversation went.

"I met Mark online. We went out a couple of times. He seemed like a good guy. I liked him enough. It's been a couple of years since I had sex. A woman has needs, you know!"

"Oh, I agree."

"We start going at it. And I tell him I like it rough. I like the intensity. I like to be submissive in the bedroom. Everywhere else in my life, I have to be in charge. I don't want to be the boss in the bedroom. I don't want to think. I just want to be told what to do. Is that bad?"

"Not at all. Sounds like you know what you want."

"We're having sex, and he's manhandling me. It's all good. I start giving him oral. He grabs my hair, and it starts to get rough. He starts ramming himself down my throat. I don't love that, but I'm okay with it. Just let a girl breath right?"

"Then, while I'm basically choking on him, he starts laughing at me. I don't know what happened. I just snapped. I have to get myself in a certain headspace to be submissive like that. I totally open myself up to go there. I couldn't believe he was laughing. I may like it rough, but I don't want to be humiliated. There's a difference."

"You're going for the intensity and excitement—not to be degraded."

"It threw me back to my abusive husband. I just got up and left. I didn't feel safe. I needed to go. I didn't know what else to do. Was that bad?"

"No. Sounds like you did the right thing to me. You need to feel safe in a situation like that. What were you feeling?"

"I was angry that I allowed him to do that to me. I felt taken advantage of. I felt humiliated."

"The situation sounds humiliating. And I want to understand how you felt humiliated."

"I felt humiliated as a woman. It reminded me of my marriage. I've endured so much humiliation in my life, Dolan. I told myself never again. That's why I got so mad. I've had it."

"When I hear people say they 'feel humiliated' it often means they didn't feel they were human."

"Yes, I felt objectified like I'm a thing and not a person. As if I don't have any feelings and he doesn't care about me at all. He didn't even apologize, which upset me too."

"I understand your anger. I wonder if underneath all the ugliness if this situation makes you feel shame? I hear that the humiliation took you straight back to your marriage. Did you flash back to your childhood abuse?"

"A little bit."

"I know this is hard but would you try and see if you feel shame? I know it sucks. But, I want you to stop feeling humiliated. Can you stop and feel if there's shame deep down?"

Fredee closes her eyes and allows herself to feel. A single tear falls from the corner of her left eye. My heart breaks.

"Yes, I feel shame."

"Let's work through the Four Simple Questions. We already answered Question 1. You feel shame. You also feel humiliation but we're not going to deal with that right now. You felt objectified and devalued, that you don't have any feelings, and that he didn't care. Let's combine all those things under 'I'm not a person.' So you make your shame mean you're not a person. Does that sound right to you?"

Fredee nods.

I read Question 3 and its statements. She agrees with all of them. We're now ready to find out what she needs to know.

Many words resonate for Fredee: *worthy, lovable, powerful, precious, beautiful, special, acceptable, safe, cautious,* and *visible.*

"You have a lot of words that resonate here. I'm going to go over your list, and I want you to tell me if the word resonates weak, medium, or strong."

"Okay."

As I read Fredee's list, she narrowed it down to the words that resonated the strongest: *precious, beautiful, special, cautious,* and *visible.*

"I'm just reading your 'strong' list so you can compare them to one another. *Precious.*"

"Strong."

"*Beautiful.*"

"Strong."

"Does beautiful resonate more than precious?"

"Well, no."

We make our way through the list until Fredee is left with *precious*. Compared to all the other words that strongly resonated, *precious* resonates the strongest.

"That's what you need to know. You are precious. You've been suffering all this time because you didn't know you are precious. You needed to know that."

"I do. I've never felt precious."

"But you are. Do you feel precious now?"

"I do. Yes."

"One final question. I'm going to ask you what the truth is. And you tell me what you just learned. You say 'I am' and then what you know now."

"What's the truth?"

"I am precious."

Next, Fredee and I went through the Healing Dialogue. The Healing Dialogue took her back to when she was a frightened, confused, and powerless child. Fredee got to hear the healing words she needed as a child. She comforted her broken heart. As she was saying the Healing Dialogue to her hurting heart, I could see her chin muscles quivering. *So strong, so loving, so brave. The truth is you are so very precious, Fredee.*

If, like Fredee, you find that many words are resonating, then rate each word: weak, medium, or strong resonation. Then compare strong word to strong word until you find the word that resonates the strongest.

Heather – Hard Time Accepting Your Truth

You've worked your way up to Question 4, and now it's time to accept your truth. But you can't. Heather's truth was "I am safe," but she still felt scared. She couldn't accept her truth despite feeling it. Like Heather, you may need to do a Healing Dialogue before you can accept your truth.

Heather is 22 years old. She drove down from Los Angeles to my office because she felt uncomfortable with herself. She was critical of her appearance. She was unhappy and always found flaws with how she looked.

Heather told me she was sexually assaulted as a teenager, an experience that left her shamed to the core.

Heather shared a recent situation that triggered shame. Her boyfriend, Tyler, came over and invited her to dinner with his parents that evening. Heather was relaxing, in full-blown lounge mode. She wasn't expecting this invitation.

Tyler convinced her to go. She didn't have much time to get ready and felt pressured. She scrambled to find something to wear, trying on several outfits, all of which, in her mind, looked bad. She couldn't decide what to wear and felt uncomfortable in her skin. She wanted to look perfect, and rushing around only made the pressure worse, triggering her shame.

Heather and I worked through the Four Simple Questions. Heather already knew that she felt shame. She made her shame mean "I'm not good enough." We moved on to discover her truth.

I began to read from the truth list and told her to sit back, close her eyes, and feel which word resonated.

Often, when a person is shamed to the core, they need to know they are *lovable, acceptable,* or that they *belong*. These words didn't resonate with Heather, so I tried a different word. From my experience, another driving force for people with deep shame is that they don't feel safe.

I ask, "Do you need to know you're safe?" Bull's-eye. Heather began to cry. Tears streamed down her face. Heather needed to know she was safe. Vulnerability and fear had ruled her life. She experienced unsafe as being uncomfortable in her own skin.

I asked her, "What's the truth?" Heather just looked at me with red eye watery eyes. I could see that she still didn't feel safe. Her truth couldn't get in because she still didn't feel safe. Discovering she needed to feel safe was an emotional experience that was both painful and validating. To feel safe, Heather needed to heal first.

Heather and I moved into the Healing Dialogue phase. I asked Heather if she had a nickname she liked growing up.

"Yes, Tweety," she replied. Heather smiled when I said we were going to talk to Tweety.

Heather sat back in her chair and closed her eyes. She put both hands over her heart to feel Tweety and give her a little hug.

"Tell Tweety you know she's been hurting."

Heather repeated those words and began crying harder. She struggled through her tears but carried on. You could see her connect to her heart. Heather's hurting heart was finally getting the love and acknowledgement that it needed.

Heather worked her way through the Healing Dialogue. She spoke with sincerity and compassion to Tweety, demonstrating tremendous courage by allowing herself to experience her suffering.

"How's Tweety doing?"

"Better," she said.

"Does Tweety believe you?"

"Yes."

The energy in the room had changed. There was now a sense of peace.

"What's the truth?" I asked.

"I am safe."

"How do you feel? Do you feel hopeful?"

"Yes, but what I really feel is relief."

Sometimes when you feel scared, it's hard to take your truth to heart, even though you know it's true. It's hard to accept because you still feel scared. This is what Heather experienced. She still felt fear after discovering her truth. The Healing Dialogue helped Heather's hurting heart hear the words it needed to hear. Her heart needed to release some pain and fear before it could feel safe. The Healing Dialogue provided the reassurance and safety her heart needed.

Fear is a natural and strong feeling. It's instinctive. Heather accepted her truth, 'I am safe,' but there was more work to do. While she felt relief, she still needed to nourish her truth. She needed to understand what feeling *safe* meant. She needed to pay attention to what made her feel unsafe and safe and to honor those feelings. This is how Heather copes, learns and grows moving forward. The good news: Heather's now much more comfortable in her skin.

Chapter 19 – Conclusion

I had procrastinated completing my fourth-grade math homework: computing the volume of a cylinder. It was now nighttime, and I was tired. I wanted my dad to help me with my math homework. But secretly, I wanted him to do it for me. My dad, a former math teacher, always took the opportunity to teach me whenever the subject arose, regardless of my convenience.

My dad explained that to find a cylinder's volume you had first to figure out the area of the circle and then multiply that by the length of the cylinder. After his explanation and working through an example, he asked if I understood. I said I did.

Then I asked, "What's the answer to the first problem?"

He answered, "You said you understand, go figure it out." My secret plan to get my dad to do my homework failed.

Fast-forward a couple of years to my sixth-grade graduation picnic. There was a guessing game: How many gumballs are in the three-foot clear plastic cylinder? Guess what I did? I looked at the bottom of the tube and counted all the gumballs in the circle. Then I counted all the gumballs lengthwise and multiplied. I won that contest thanks to my dad teaching me how to calculate the volume of a cylinder.

Knowledge is only truly powerful when you apply it.

You have learned to feel your feelings, the Four Simple Questions, and the Healing Dialogue. You have learned Shame Hack. You have learned the formula. Now, it's time to apply it.

Feelings that bother you are your cylinder of gumballs, a solvable problem if you take the time to figure it out. Nothing stands between you and liberating yourself from shame.

It's time to claim your heart and own your future. No more living in fear of your feelings. No more shame. Feel free. Feel peace. Feel understood. Understand yourself now. Dig into the present. There is nothing to wait for. Enjoy the discoveries. Enjoy yourself. Go forth and hack away. You're worth it!

Afterward – Help Wanted

What would the world look like if people hacked their shame instead of taking it out on themselves or others?

Here's a big idea: If we do the hacking work now, perhaps future generations won't have to live in shame. There was no one to model resolving shame when you were a kid. You did the best you could. But when you learned Shame Hack, you became a potential model. You become part of the solution, as does anyone you turn on to Shame Hack.

My dream is to have people from around the world contribute their truths. I would love to see people from other countries and cultures discovering the same truths. We could see that perhaps we are not so different after all. Our truths transcend geography, age, race, gender, income, culture, and sexual orientation. Your truth may resonate with someone you never met who lives on the opposite side of the globe, or their truth may resonate with you.

So if Shame Hack helped you (and I hope it did), you can help others by sharing your experience.

How to share?

Tell your friends and family. When people comment on the difference in you (and they will), share your experience. Offer them hope that they, too, could heal their shame. You never know how sharing your experience and authentically relating, seeing, or understanding someone may influence their life.

Share your "I am _____" truths on my website www.shamehack.com and on other social media (#shamehack). Make a video, take a selfie, write, draw, or text - especially the truths that aren't already on the list.

Contribute your story. Write up what happened when you learned the Four Simple Questions and submit it on my website www.shamehack.com.

Donate copies of Shame Hack to your local library.

References

The questions that make up the Four Simple Questions are not my brain child. They have their roots in cognitive behavioral therapy (CBT). What *is* my brain child is how I have put them together and the way you answer them. You are not using the questions to examine aberrant thinking. You're using the questions to reveal what's driving your feeling. CBT moves you from your feelings to your head. Shame Hack has you stay in your feelings looking for the suffering that propels them.

Shame Hack uses a concept from Viktor Frankl, in that you are finding meaning in your suffering. But where Frankl comes from more of an existential perspective, Shame Hack comes from a feeling place.

Shame Hack has ties to inner child therapy. There's a flavor of re-parenting in the Healing Dialogue.

Lastly, Shame Hack expanded on the idea of active listening from the book *Parent Effectiveness Training* by Thomas Gordon. Active listening between parent and child became active empathy between you and your heart. Demonstrating you understand how your heart feels was derived from this book.

Gordon, Thomas. *Parent Effectiveness Training*. Three Rivers Press, 2000.

Lickel, Brian, et al. *The Self-Conscious Emotions – Group Conscious Emotions*. Guilford Press, 2007, p.353. (Chapter 8, p. 98)

Korb, Alex and Daniel Siegel. *Upward Spiral – Using Neuroscience to Reverse the Course of Depression, One Small Change at a Time*. New Harbinger Publication, 2015. (Chapter 8 p. 99)

Breines, Julia G., et al., *Self-compassion as a predictor of interleukin-6 response to acute psychosocial stress*, Brain, Behavior and Immunity, 2014. (Chapter 16, p. 218)

About the Author

Have you ever heard someone say something that stirs something deep inside you? This is exactly what happened to me while watching a short documentary on David McCullough, historian and Pulitzer prize winner. McCullough says something that unexpectedly touches deep in my heart.

In his gentle way he is talking about his aspiration when he writes history. He mentions that he doesn't just want his historical writing to be readable, or interesting. He says, "I want it to be something that moves the reader. That moves me." When I hear him say this I feel like I've been found when I didn't even know was lost. His words stir a longing inside me. I didn't realize it but I want to move people too. I want to be moved. I want to make people feel something. Something meaningful. Something good.

I am curious about human nature and what people feel and experience. To me one to the best things is seeing a person discover their truth. I love it when the epiphany hits and the truth rings out. A person realizes they are lovable, safe, or belongs. It's a precious moment.

I dream big. I dream that Shame Hack will bring people together from around the world. When people share their story with someone many miles away and they relate. In this way you can see that people have similar feelings and stories all the world over. I hope this connection shrinks the world a bit and makes it a little more loving and compassionate place.

I live in San Diego. One of my favorite actives to do there is swim in the ocean with friends. I enjoy trying different restaurants. I also like to catch a show when they come through town. I enjoy cooking and learning to make new dishes. To me good food is love.

Made in the USA
Lexington, KY
22 August 2019